# THE
# GOLF
# LOVER'S GUIDE TO
# SCOTLAND

Michael Whitehead

WHITE OWL

AN IMPRINT OF PEN & SWORD BOOKS LTD.
YORKSHIRE – PHILADELPHIA

First published in Great Britain
PEN & SWORD WHITE OWL
An imprint of
Pen & Sword Books Ltd
Yorkshire - Philadelphia

Copyright © Michael Whitehead

ISBN 9781526733771

The right of Michael Whitehead to be identified as
Author of this work has been asserted by him in
accordance with the Copyright, Designs and Patents Act
1988. A CIP catalogue record for this book is available
from the British Library.

Printed and bound in India by Replika Press Pvt. Ltd.
Design: Paul Wilkinson.

Pen & Sword Books Limited incorporates the imprints
of Atlas, Archaeology, Aviation, Discovery, Family
History, Fiction, History, Maritime, Military, Military
Classics, Politics, Select, Transport, True Crime, Air
World, Frontline Publishing, Leo Cooper, Remember
When, Seaforth Publishing,  The Praetorian Press,
Wharncliffe Local History, Wharncliffe Transport,
Wharncliffe True Crime and White Owl.

For a complete list of Pen & Sword titles please contact
PEN & SWORD BOOKS LIMITED
47 Church Street, Barnsley, South Yorkshire, S70 2AS,
United Kingdom
E-mail: enquiries@pen-and-sword.co.uk
Website: www.pen-and-sword.co.uk

Or
PEN AND SWORD BOOKS
1950 Lawrence Rd, Havertown, PA 19083, USA
E-mail: Uspen-and-sword@casematepublishers.com
Website: www.penandswordbooks.com

# CONTENTS

# INTRODUCTION

## ABOUT THIS GUIDE

For anyone planning a golfing trip to Scotland, with over 550 courses to choose from, deciding which to play during your visit can be a daunting task. The majority of the courses within this guide will be well known to many, with the addition of a few hidden gems, and likely be on your wishlist of those you would love to play before you hang up your golf clubs. (Do any of us ever really retire from this beautiful game, though?)

The main section of this guide is devoted to some of Scotland's finest, and most acclaimed 18-hole golf courses available for visitors to play. Within each dedicated chapter, you will find everything you need including all the essential course information, contact details, how to book a round and just as important – <u>when</u> you can book a round as a visitor.. There is also information about the rich history of each course and its club along with a useful outline of how best to approach playing the course.

While the main focus of each chapter is on the primary course for which they are renowned, a lot of the clubs within this guide have a number of other courses also available for visitors to play. The details of these courses are outlined towards the end of the chapter along with a selection of other courses in the area within easy travelling distance.

In addition to the 18-hole chapters, there is also a section dedicated to some of Scotland's most cherished 9-hole courses and two special chapters: one for a unique 12-hole course and one for the oldest golf course of them all. For for those of you who like to play as often and over as many layouts as possible there's plenty to digest.

# Acknowledgements

I'D LIKE TO THANK the following people, who gave up their valuable time to ensure each course chapter was accurate and up to date. Their cooperation and communication were greatly appreciated:

Gordon Hay (Boat Of Garten Golf Club), Keir McNicoll and Kierran Allardice (Carnoustie Golf Links), Stuart McColm and Stefanie Whyte (Castle Stuart Golf Links), Elaine Johnson and David Snodgrass (Crail Golfing Society), Les Durno and Neil Murray (Cruden Bay Golf Club), Ian Ferguson (Dundonald Links), Gary Silcock, Billy Murray and David Blackadder (Gleneagles), Alan Mackie, Ronnie Sinclair and Charles Birrell (Golf House Club, Elie), Stuart Bendoris (Gullane Golf Club), Audrey Hogg and Alan Hogg (Kingsbarns Golf Links), Margaret Wylie (The Machrihanish Golf Club), Stuart McEwen (HCEG – Muirfield), Fraser Cromarty (The Nairn Golf Club), Mary Lou Watkins and Martyn Huish (North Berwick Golf Club), Ken Goodwin (Prestwick Golf Club), Sandra Nicholson and David Ross (Royal Aberdeen), Neil Hampton (Royal Dornoch), Robert McInnes (Royal Troon), Robert Kennedy (Southerness Golf Club), Kat Keith, Laurie Watson and Steve North (St Andrews), Kate Brewer and Steve Wilson (Trump International Golf Links), Ricky Hall and Lynsey Mcilwraith (Trump Turnberry), Douglas Zuill (Western Gailes Golf Club), Pietre Johnston (Shiskine Golf & Tennis Club), Jennifer Jarvis and Kenny Armstrong (Musselburgh Links), David Gallacher and Janet Thomson (Anstruther Golf Club), Annie Wallom and Ian Grieve (Bridge of Allan Golf Club), Bill Baird (Carrbridge Golf Club), Andrew Thomson (Comrie Golf Club), Lizzie Stevens, Dick Lewis and David Stewart (Killin Golf Club), Gordon Hibbert (St Fillans Golf Club).

I'd also like to thank Peter Kane (System2), for coordinating discussions between myself and certain Clubs with whom he works alongside, Mark Alexander (www.markalexandergolfphotography.com) who kindly permitted the use of his wonderful photographs, Neil Laird whose website (www.scottishgolfhistory.org) provided so much insightful information on the history of many courses within this guide and, finally, Ian and Lorraine Devenish for their tremendous hospitality during my stay at Cruden Bay B&B which even included a lift to my next appointment at Trump International Golf Links. Your courtesy shown to my son and myself made our visit to such a beautiful part of the world all the more amazing – thank you.

To my wife, Kellie and our children; Hermione, Charlie and James. Thank you for your love and support and for never growing tired of listening to my golf stories.

All the course chapters in both the 18-hole and 9-hole sections are listed alphabetically. This guide was written with the assistance of the day-to-day management at each Club or Golf Links who have all confirmed and endorsed the accuracy of each course chapter.

Here are some general points to consider when reading through the guide:

**Green fees**. The bandings below are for indication purposes only, based on 2019 prices, and are usually subject to change on an annual basis. It's recommended to check the actual course website or contact the club directly to confirm the precise green fee for the time of year you're planning to book.

**Price Guide: 18-hole courses**
▼ up to £99
▼ £100 – £149
▼ £150 – £200
▼ over £200

**Price Guide: 9-hole courses**
▼ up to £15
▼ £16 – £25
▼ £26 – £40

**High Season**. Typically between May and September.
**Shoulder Season**. Typically April and October.
**Low Season**. Typically November to March.

**Distance/yardage**. The measurements given for the length of each course, and longest/shortest holes, are generally from the shortest to the longest tee-boxes. All distances are in yards (yds). In some cases, the longest tees are reserved for championships or members only. Most courses have a wide selection of tees available and the starter at the course will offer advice, based on your handicap, as to which tee you should use. For a more enjoyable round, it is wise to heed this advice.

**Handicap certificate**. While a lot of courses with a handicap policy have a laid-back approach to checking certificates, and may not even ask for them, it is better to be safe than sorry and have it with you. The key is not necessarily the handicap of a particular player but more the necessity to maintain the pace of play on the course and an expectation to keep up to that.

**Caddies**. If you book a caddie be aware that, generally, they work on a self-employed basis and expect to be paid directly in cash. The amount of gratuity is entirely up to you but around 20 per cent would usually be the minimum starting point.

**Equipment hire**. Most courses have a range of equipment you would expect – pull trolleys, clubs, shoes etc. If you require a buggy for health and medical reasons it is advised to book in advance, as there will be a limited number available. The equipment hire prices quoted are based on 2019 tariffs and may be subject to change on an annual basis.

**Dress Code**. If you're planning on dining in the clubhouse before or after your round it's best to check whether there are any rules on attire before you travel.

**Tee-time**. Ensure you arrive at least thirty minutes before your tee-time in order to finalise any outstanding points regarding your booking (payments etc.). Most courses have practice facilities for you to warm up before you head to the first tee.

**Honesty Box**. A number of courses across Scotland are operated by a gallant army of unpaid volunteers and, as such, there may be times when the clubhouse and starter huts have to be left unattended. In such circumstances these courses will leave a box for golfers to pop their green fees into. So, if you turn up and there's nobody around, make sure you do the right thing.

## A BRIEF HISTORY OF GOLF

For anyone who's ever visited Edinburgh Castle, one of the must-see artefacts is the magnificently named, 500-year-old cannon, 'Mons Meg'. It sits, proudly, on a terrace in front of St Margaret's Chapel. A gift from Phillip III, Duke Of Burgundy, to his niece's husband King James II Of Scotland in 1457.

*Mons Meg.*

James II was quite fond of weaponry so the mammoth siege gun, or 'bombard', was well received and well used. James was known as 'Fiery Face' due both to his temperament and also to a distinctive facial birthmark. Coming to the throne at the age of 6, James' enthusiasm for all things military would be well timed later in his reign as he battled with the Douglases and those pesky neighbours to the south.

Inevitably, it was his love of heavy artillery that would eventually be his undoing. Standing too close to a cannon called 'the Lion' prior to the Battle of Roxburgh Castle in 1460, it exploded upon firing and killed him almost instantly.

Three years before his death, around the same time James was taking delivery of his new gift, so enraged with the lack of focus he witnessed from his troops, the king introduced an Act of Parliament banning any leisure activity in order for more rigorous archery practice. The two leisure activities that were the biggest nuisance – football and golf.

*James II Of Scotland was responsible for banning football and golf.*

And so it came to pass on 6 March 1457 the first written evidence of the game of golf in Scotland. A translation from the Act reads as follows:–

> Item, it is ordained and the decreed that the lords and barons both spiritual and temporal should organise archery displays four times in the year. And that football and golf should be utterly condemned and stopped. And that a pair of targets should be made up at all parish churches and shooting should be practiced each Sunday.... And concerning football and golf, we ordain that [those found playing these games] be punished by the local barons and, failing them, by the King's officers.

(1457 Act of Parliament. Source: www.digital.nls.uk)

Over 500 years later it's hard to imagine a more undignified entrance into history for such a revered and much loved sport. Subsequent records suggest golf continued to have a fanatical following even during those turbulent times. Further Acts under two different monarchs (James III and IV respectively), in 1470 and 1491, were required to re-affirm the original Act banning the activity.

It was not until 1502 and the signing of the Treaty of Perpetual Peace by James IV, bringing peace between England and Scotland, that golf could be played without fear of reprisal. The king himself caught the bug with the first recorded purchase of golf equipment from a Perth bow-maker.

From then on golf's popularity could not be abated. In 1553, following the first recorded evidence of play there, the Archbishop of St Andrews issued a decree allowing the local community the right to play golf on the nearby coastal sand dunes and rising, ridged, ground. Nowadays we refer to such areas as 'links'.

Golf's relationship with royalty would continue to blossom. According to legend, Mary, Queen of Scots, was a visitor to Musselburgh Links, thus regarded as the first ever female golfer. This distinction is somewhat disputed, however, as she was accused by her rivals of playing golf a day or so after her husband's death. Such a callous act was seen as clear evidence of her part in his murder.

Mary is also accredited with introducing the usage of caddies. Deriving from the French pronunciation of the word 'cadet' following her exile in France whereby young cadets would carry the clubs for the players.

Charles I was informed of the Irish rebellion while enjoying a chip-up at Leith. He would then launch into an offensive that would become known as the English Civil War. But first, the king would finish his round of golf.

Contrary to popular opinion, it was a course created in Leith rather than St Andrews that would move golf from genteel pastime to an official competitive sport. The first international golf match took place there in 1682 when the Duke Of York and his playing partner emerged victorious versus two English counterparts.

*Mary, Queen of Scots is regarded as the first female golfer.*

In 1744 the Gentleman Golfers of Leith created the first set of written rules for golf along with an annual competition. Duncan Forbes, a highly respected Lord Advocate, would draw up the rules. These regulations would be used by St Andrews ten years later when forming The St Andrews Society of Golfers. A further ten years would pass before the creation of the first ever 18-hole course at the site in 1764.

*The famous Swilcan Bridge at the Old Course, St. Andrews.*

King William IV, another regal who was keen on teeing-up, bestowed the 'Royal' title upon the Perth Golfing Society in 1833. Not to be outdone, one year later he would grant the 'Royal and Ancient' title upon the St Andrews Society of Golfers. So, in 1834, the Royal and Ancient Golf Club of St Andrews was established, becoming the most widely recognised Golf Club in the world.

As the British Empire continued its march across the globe it brought golf along for the ride. Bangalore, India opened the first Golf Club outside Europe in 1820. Clubs in Australia and South Africa would follow. Prestwick Golf Club hosted the very first Open Championship in 1860, won by Willie Park and giving rise to the first legends of the game – Old Tom Morris and his son, Young Tom Morris, would win the tournament eight times between them.

The Saint Andrews Golf Club of New York, formed in 1888, was the foundation for, quite possibly, the most passionate love affair between a nation and the sport of kings. The USGA was formed in 1894 and by 1900 over 1,000 golf clubs had been created across the country. A century later there is no doubt the USA is at the forefront of the professional game, nevertheless its heart will always be in Scotland.

## GOLFING IN SCOTLAND

With new, state-of-the-art, courses opening all across the world, golf is a sport very much in its prime. The latest technological developments are creating course layouts that are much longer and more challenging than anything we've seen before.

But as impressive as these new courses are, they are all missing one vital ingredient. It is a component so simple for all to see but one that cannot be bought. The absent feature is utterly priceless and it is this – time.

Time is what has made golfing in Scotland special. The history is special, the courses are special and the locations are special. The courses in Scotland seem so at one with their habitat, if we didn't know anything about their history, we could be forgiven for imagining they were heaven sent and humanity played no part in their construction.

Thankfully we know an awful lot about golf's proud heritage and its roots are planted firmly within Scotland's borders. We know some very fine Scottish-born men were responsible not just for the courses spread across the land, but for the pioneering work that shaped the equipment we use, and the modern-day rules we follow, from the moment we stand on the first tee to our final putt on the 18th green.

Two of the finest men were Old Tom Morris and James Braid (two names you will see very often throughout this guide). Both men were born in Fife and both began their fascination with golf in their youth as club makers. Morris, widely regarded as the father of the game, was Allan Robertson's finest student and, by all accounts, the pair were unbeatable on the course. James Braid moved to London to ply his trade before becoming a professional golfer in 1896, and in 1901, he was a founder member of the Professional Golfer's Association. Between them, Morris and Braid would win The Open Championship nine times.

After their playing days were over, these men became the original pioneers of golf course architecture, responsible for producing or redesigning over 250 courses throughout the United Kingdom. Some of these courses are among the finest

Scotland has to offer – Royal Dornoch, Carnoustie, Cruden Bay, Prestwick, Gleneagles and Royal Troon to name just a few.

The history of these courses is fascinating and is as much an attraction for visitors as the courses themselves. Stories of Mary, Queen of Scots, swinging her clubs around Musselburgh Links and Robert The Bruce's decision to destroy Turnberry Castle lest it fall into the advancing English army's possession. Scotland's glorious heritage is intertwined with its golf courses in a way other countries could only dream of.

It is not only the courses that are famous all over the world; some of the most revered holes are to be found here too. The original Redan, the most plagiarised hole in golf, proudly resides on the West Links at North Berwick. The Road hole at St Andrews, where so many golfers' dreams of holding aloft the Claret Jug have faded in the cavernous bunker at the front of the green.

Standing on the 9th tee at Cruden Bay with Slains Castle in the distance and the entire course spread out beneath you, leaves you with a sense of having walked along a stairway to golfing heaven.

When you play golf anywhere else in the world it's just you versus the course. In Scotland, it's you versus the golfing gods and whatever your score, there will only be one winner – you.

## WHAT MAKES A GREAT GOLF EXPERIENCE?

There's an undeniable truth that sets golf apart from all other mainstream sports. For example, if you love football and you wanted to be able to say, on your deathbed, that you've played the beautiful game across all habitable continents, then there's no doubt it would be an experience of a lifetime. However, while the elements may be different, each offering a unique challenge, a football pitch is still a football pitch wherever you play. The dimensions are exactly the same in Buenos Aires as they are in Manchester. Two nets at each end, two 18yd boxes with a penalty spot and one big centre circle. It's exactly the same, wherever you are. Cricket? Same. Rugby? Same.

## Golf? Different.

Every golf course around the globe has one thing in common – they are all unique. No two courses are ever the same. Golf is the only major sport that offers a totally different experience wherever you go.

So, how does a golf course achieve greatness? If there were a poll of golf lovers asking them to name just one course they could play before they died, it's highly likely most would choose between Augusta National and the Old Course, St Andrews. But does prestige and pedigree automatically translate into a fun golfing experience? If a high handicapper had to play Augusta twice a week their love for the game would surely begin to wane. After all, fishing your ball out of the water can become a little tedious after a while, regardless of whether it's at Amen Corner or your local pitch and putt.

The unique status of every golf course makes defining what makes a golf course great nigh on impossible. This is mainly due to greatness being very much in the eye of the beholder. Course designers constantly battle with a formula that creates a sufficient challenge for low handicappers while providing a happy experience for the average golfer.

Golf can best be described as a patchwork quilt of an experience. A round at St Andrews or Carnoustie would be something you would never forget, but if you did it on your own, through howling wind and driving rain, could you honestly say its been more enjoyable than a round at your local golf club with good friends in beaming sunshine where you shoot -4 under your handicap?

Maybe the course isn't so important? Perhaps what matters the most is the company as you go round? Maybe it's the view from the 1st tee or the challenge of a particular hole?

As a keen but distinctly average golfer, I just like to have fun on the course. And I like golf courses that are fun. If I'm sat in a clubhouse after a round, and I'm already looking forward to the next one regardless of where that may be, I know it's been a great day.

# 18-HOLE COURSES

## BOAT OF GARTEN GOLF CLUB

Boat of Garten Golf & Tennis Club,
Nethybridge Road,
Boat of Garten,
PH24 3BQ
**www.boatgolf.com**
**Phone:** +44 (0) 1479 831282
**Email:** office@boatgolf.com

**Essential course details –**
**Par:** 70 (White tees) / 72 (Red tees)
**S.S.S:** 69 (White tees) / 71 (Red tees)
**Slope rating:** Not available
**Length:** 5,093yds–5,837yds
**Longest hole:** Par-5 4th, 469yds–513yds
**Shortest hole:** Par-3 9th, 137yds–152yds
**Type:** Heathland/Moorland

**Handicap Certificate:** Not required

**Green fees:**
▼ per person per round
▼ junior per round (under-18)

**Caddies:** Available upon specific request

**Equipment hire:**
£30 – buggy
£25 – clubs
£10 – electric trolley
£5 – push trolley

**How do I book a round of golf?**
There are three ways to book a round of golf at Boat of Garten Golf Club:

*Online:*
www.boatgolf.com (register for booking)

*Phone:*
+44 (0) 1479 831282

*Email:*
office@boatgolf.com (include all relevant details – preferred dates/times, group size etc)

## HISTORY

The course at Boat of Garten dates back to 1898 when the layout consisted of just six holes. Players would have to wait over thirty years before the course was extended to a full eighteen. In 1910, another two holes were added to the original six, then in 1930, James Braid was asked to re-design the course and bring it up to eighteen holes after additional land became available.

It would take a further two years

Fairway leading to the green at the 2nd hole, a favourite amongst many who visit Boat of Garten, with the snow-capped Cairngorms in the distance.
*Boat of Garten Golf & Tennis Club.*

for the club committee to agree to the extra rent and to Braid's plans before the full 18-hole course was available to play in 1932. Braid's course layout remained untouched until the 1980s when the 14th hole was relocated with the addition of a dogleg fairway. At the beginning of the '90s the club was finally able to buy the land on which the course sits.

At the beginning of this century there were further changes to the 1st and 5th holes with both receiving improved greens. The 13th was later renovated and changed from a par-4 to a par-5. The most recent changes were to the clubhouse which included new locker rooms and a new Pro shop.

## PLAYING THE COURSE

'The Boat' is set among some of the most awe-inspiring scenery you will find anywhere in Scotland. The River Spey runs alongside the course, in the heart of the Cairngorms National Park. Beyond the river are the Monadhliath Mountains and to the south are the stunning Cairngorms. As you reach the first tee you're left in no doubt why Boat of Garten is known as the gateway to the Highlands. This is a setting that will live long in the memory.

Regarded as one of the hardest, quirkiest and most fun courses under 6,000 total yards. Long hitters will probably be okay leaving their driver in the bag but make no mistake, this is a high quality Braid layout where all 18 holes have a real unique feel to them.

The course starts with the nightmare scenario all golfers dread: a par-3. With out of bounds along the right and two bunkers on the left, aim your tee-shot towards the right-hand side of the green although be careful, as there is a partly hidden bunker on that side too.

Despite being a relatively short par-4, the 2nd hole has previously been named one of the best 100 golf holes in the UK. This is followed by another par-3, which is all carry, as anything short could roll down the steep right-hand slope. The 4th is the first par-5 and an opportunity to hit the green in two if you can reach beyond the hill on the fairway.

**6 ) SIGNATURE HOLE: PAR-4 6TH, 314–403YDS, 'AVENUE'.**
After a short par-4 5th you come to one of the best holes on the course, a tricky, par-4, dogleg right that requires both a solid tee-shot and approach to reach the green. If you can't make it in two, leave your approach to the left of the green, as there is generally an easier pitch from here than from the right side.

Two more par-4s follow before the shortest hole on the course at the 9th. As with the 3rd, this hole also requires all carry if you're to avoid a steep slope away to the left.

The 10th sounds like an easy hole on paper (266-yard, par-4) and is definitely driveable for those capable. However, danger lurks on all sides and anyone aiming straight at the green from the tee runs the risk of finding trees on the left as the ground slopes steeply in this direction. There's no harm in playing conservatively and laying up for a pitch on to the green, just don't get caught in two minds.

The next two holes are both par-4s with the 12th in particular offering outstanding views southwards. James Braid himself declared, 'I don't think there is any equals it', and who would argue with him. The 13th is the last par-5 on the course. Here, you'll find your tee-shot tends to run to the right, and the second shot needs to be arrow straight if it is to find the fairway, allowing

**Picturesque view down the fairway towards the green from the 12th tee. It's easy to see why it was a favourite of James Braid.**
*Boat of Garten Golf & Tennis Club.*

**View from the top of the gully at the 15th hole.** *GoodSundays.com*

a short pitch to the green. A three-shot par-5 for sure.

The 15th is without doubt the quirkiest hole on the course. It gets its name (Gully) from the deep depression, which lies between 180–230yds from the tee. So, you're left with a decision to make – do you go for it? Both making it over and playing short will leave you a clear sight of the green, but landing right at the bottom will leave you a very difficult shot to make it out.

You're given some assistance from the tee-box in the form of a lookout tower that allows you to survey the layout of the hole before you hit your drive.

Hole 16 is a deceptive par-3 that appears much longer than it actually is. Trust your instincts and club selection, as this requires yet another all-carry tee-shot. The 17th is a short par-4 offering excellent views over the course and a chance to pick up a shot.

And finally, a course that starts with a tricky par-3 ends with a par-4 that can easily play as a par-5. The line for your tee-shot at the 18th is the clubhouse door. Any approach shots that don't quite make it to the green will likely hit the front slope, which will ensure the ball will roll back at least 20yds. Anything over the green usually finds trouble. A par here is certainly one to savour.

## CARNOUSTIE GOLF LINKS – CHAMPIONSHIP COURSE

Carnoustie Golf Centre,
Links Parade,
Carnoustie,
DD7 7JE
**www.carnoustiegolflinks.co.uk**
**Phone:** +44 (0) 1241 802270 (General) / +44 (0) 1241 802290 (Starter's Box)
**Email:** golf@carnoustiegolflinks.co.uk

**Essential course details –**
**Par:** 72 (White tees) / 70 (Red tees)
**S.S.S:** 75 (White) / 71 (Red)
**Slope rating:** 139 (White) / 130 (Red)
**Length:** 6,144yds–6,948yds
**Longest hole:** Par-5 6th 'Hogan's Alley', 485yds–520yds
**Shortest hole:** par-3 13th 'Whins', 118yds–161yds
**Type:** Links

**Handicap Certificate:** Required (maximum handicap is 28 for men and 36 for ladies).

**Green fees:**
▼ Adult per round
▼ Junior per round (14yr–18yrs inclusive)

*Winter prices* – 50 per cent of summer fees. During this period mats must be used at all times on the fairways.

**Caddies:**
£55 per round (+ gratuity).
Book in advance (at least 24 hours beforehand): caddiemaster@carnoustiegolflinks.co.uk or phone 0044 (0) 1241 802288.

**Equipment hire:**
£5 - push trolleys

**How do I book a round of golf?**
Carnoustie Golf Links offers tee-time priority to affiliated club members, however, visitor bookings are available for the Championship Course at the following times during the week:

| | |
|---|---|
| *Monday–Friday* | *9.00 am–12.30 pm & 1.30 pm–4.00 pm* |
| *Saturday* | *2.00 pm onwards* |
| *Sunday* | *11.30 am onwards* |

There are three ways to book a round at Carnoustie Golf Links (advance booking is essential) -

*Online:*
www.carnoustiegolflinks.co.uk/booking

*Email:*
golf@carnoustiegolflinks.co.uk (include all relevant details – preferred dates/times, group size etc)

*Phone:*
+44 (0) 1241 802270

## HISTORY

Sir Robert Maule's obituary, written in 1560, notes that he was a gentleman of high standing in the community and one who enjoyed a wager while playing his beloved 'gowf' on Barry Links – an area near to the current course location. If he lost the game he would retreat to the local pub and buy everyone a drink. So, the next time you and your friends suggest 'loser buys the drinks' after your usual 18 holes, you can recall this popular custom has its origins in Carnoustie folklore.

Very little is noted of the course's development over the next 300 years until the formation of The Carnoustie Golf Club in 1839. Originally a 10-hole course until Old Tom Morris was brought in to assist his elder brother, George, and create an 18-hole course in 1867. A year later the Dalhousie Golf Club was created, followed by Carnoustie Ladies Golf Club in 1873 (the oldest ladies club in the world).

The course would have to wait until 1931 before hosting its first Open Championship, won by Tommy Armour, and was the location of legendary US golfer Ben Hogan's only Open appearance – and victory by four shots – in 1953. Other notable winners of the Claret Jug at Carnoustie include Gary Player in 1968 and Tom Watson in 1975.

Prior to Paul Lawrie's stunning win in 1999, the Carnoustie Hotel was opened overlooking the 1st and 18th holes – the only hotel in the world to offer such a view of a championship course. In 2018 further developments were made, in anticipation of The Open Championship; won emphatically by Franceso Molinari, with the creation of a new £5 million Golf Performance Centre.

## PLAYING THE COURSE

Usually when you're en route to a course you might be thinking to yourself: 'have I forgotten anything?' Clubs – check. Shoes – check. Plenty of spare balls – check. When you play The Championship Course at Carnoustie, if you forget everything else, you must remember one thing – your A-game!

There is no hiding place on this course, no trees lining the fairway to protect you from the howling North Sea wind as it blows in from the Tay estuary. This is raw, wild, links golf from the first tee to the final approach into the 18th green over the infamous Barry Burn.

**Aerial view of the 18th green and 1st fairway taken from The Carnoustie Golf Hotel.** *Carnoustie Golf Links.*

Carnoustie is, without doubt, one of the sternest tests a golfer will face. However, it is one that should be faced with relish and one that can bring immense pleasure and enjoyment. So, are you ready?

First things first – if you've never played the course before and are a double figure handicapper, go from the yellow tees. In effect this will leave you with only one par-5 on the course but it's the only one you'll need.

One description often missing about this course is its fairness. There are no tricks here. No blind spots off the tee, no wild bounces off the green (they're all pretty flat), no hidden hazards ready to jump out and swallow your ball. This course doesn't need them. What you see in front of you when sizing up your shot is what you have to deal with. It's all on you.

The first five holes are actually pretty straightforward. All par-4s, a couple with doglegs to the right and with most of the trouble towards the front of the greens, so an opportunity to hit the ball to the back.

Then it's on to your first real test.

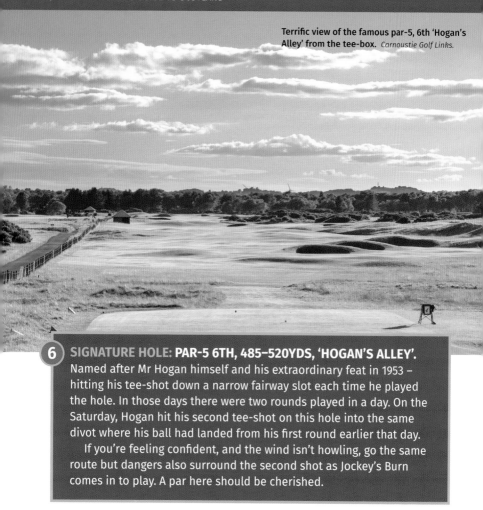

Terrific view of the famous par-5, 6th 'Hogan's Alley' from the tee-box. *Carnoustie Golf Links.*

**6** **SIGNATURE HOLE: PAR-5 6TH, 485–520YDS, 'HOGAN'S ALLEY'.**
Named after Mr Hogan himself and his extraordinary feat in 1953 – hitting his tee-shot down a narrow fairway slot each time he played the hole. In those days there were two rounds played in a day. On the Saturday, Hogan hit his second tee-shot on this hole into the same divot where his ball had landed from his first round earlier that day.

If you're feeling confident, and the wind isn't howling, go the same route but dangers also surround the second shot as Jockey's Burn comes in to play. A par here should be cherished.

The back-9 holes at Carnoustie are regarded as possibly the most difficult in the world. Lots of very long par-4s requiring focus and accuracy off the tee. The 15th, 16th and 17th in particular are seen as the most challenging closing holes a golfer will face. The 16th is a 245-yard par-3, so if you fancy taking your driver out you're in good company – Jack Nicklaus used it here in 1968, finishing in second place overall that year behind Gary Player.

Finally to the 18th, where you'll find the official caddies' notes state anything lower than a seven should be rewarded with a stiff drink in the

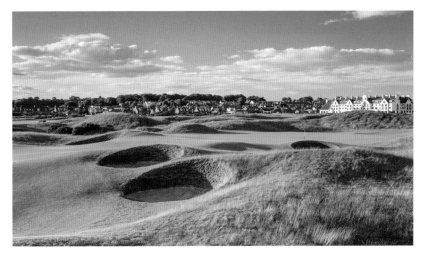

**The par-4 15th green with the Golf Hotel and Carnoustie village in the background.** *Carnoustie Golf Links.*

clubhouse. Just remember, if it goes horribly wrong right at the end, Jean Van de Velde (1999) and Johnny Miller's (1975) hopes of lifting the claret jug came crashing down at the same spot.

# Other courses on site

In addition to the Championship Course, Carnoustie Golf Links also has the following courses available for visitors to play:

● **BURNSIDE COURSE (18 HOLES)**
Regarded as a very fine test of links golf in its own right with some of the short holes regarded as every bit as challenging as any you'll find on a typical championship standard course.

**Par:** 68 (Yellow tees) / 71 (Red tees)
**S.S.S:** 70 (Yellow tees) / 72 (Red tees)
**Length:** 5,400yds–6,028yds

Green fees:
▼ Adult per round
▼ Junior per round
▼ Juvenile per round (under-14)

● **BUDDON LINKS COURSE (18 HOLES)**
Opened in 1979, designed by Peter Alliss and Dave Thomas. Recently had a $1 million renovation specifically introducing two new holes.

**Par:** 68 (White tees) / 67 (Red tees)
**S.S.S:** 69 (White & Red tees)
**Length:** 5,035yds–5,921yds

**Green fees:**
▼ Adult per round
▼ Junior per round
▼ Juvenile per round (under-14)

As with the championship course,

winter fees (November 2018–March 2019) are 50 per cent of summer prices.

### ● THE NESTIE (6 HOLES)
New junior course opened in May 2014. Free for all to play – members or non-members. You can use clubs from the Pro shop in the Golf Centre.

# 18-hole courses nearby

### ● ARBROATH GOLF LINKS
Old Tom Morris (1877) and James Braid (1931) both had a hand in the design of Arbroath Links course.

**Website:** www.arbroathgolfcourse.co.uk
**Email:** lindsay.ewart@btconnect.com
**Telephone:** +44 (0) 1241 875837

**Par:** 70 (White & Red tees)
**Length:** 5,377yds–6,200yds
**Type:** Links

**Fees:**
▼ per round (weekday & weekend)

### ● DOWNFIELD GOLF CLUB
Less than thirty minutes from Carnoustie, Paul Lawrie described Downfield as one of the finest inland courses in the UK.

**Website:** www.downfieldgolf.com
**Email:** downfieldgc@aol.com
**Telephone:** +44 (0) 1382 825595
**Par:** 72 (Blue tees) / 74 (Red tees)
**Length:** 5,839yds–6,560yds
**Type:** Parkland

**Fees:**
▼ per round (weekday & weekend)

### ● PANMURE GOLF CLUB

Tight fairways, challenging carries and compact, undulating greens make this course a tough test with a great combination of both links and heath elements.

**Website:** www.panmuregolfclub.co.uk
**Email:** professional@panmuregolfclub.co.uk
**Telephone:** +44 (0) 1241 852460 (or 855120)
**Par:** 70 (Yellow tees) / 74 (Red tees)
**Length:** 5,684yds–6,113yds
**Type:** Links

**Fees:**
▼\*: per round (May–September)

\* = Visitor tee-times are available any time except Tuesday before 1.30 pm and Saturday before 3.00 pm

### ● MONIFIETH GOLF CLUB – MEDAL COURSE

Opened in 1858, previously held final qualifying for The Open Championship. A good test for all standards of golfer.

**Website:** www.monifiethgolfclub.co.uk
**Email:** bookings@monifiethlinks.com
**Telephone:** +44 (0) 1382 532767

**Par:** 71 (White tees) / 73 (Red tees)
**Length:** 5,972yds–6,655yds
**Type:** Links

**Fees:**
▼ per round (April–October 2018)

## CASTLE STUART GOLF LINKS

Castle Stuart Golf Links,
Inverness,
IV2 7JL,
Scotland
**www.castlestuartgolf.com**
**Phone:** +44 (0) 1463 796111
**Email:** bookings@castlestuartgolf.com

Essential course details –
**Par:** 72 (All tees)
**S.S.S:** 73 (White tees) / 71 (Red tees)
**Slope rating:** 135 (White tees) / 127 (Red tees)
**Length:** 5,148yds–6,553yds
**Longest hole:** Par-5 18th, 420yds–595yds
**Shortest hole:** Par-3 11th, 91yds–144yds
**Type:** Links

**Handicap Certificate:** Not required
**Green fees:**
▼ per round (Shoulder season)
▼ per round (High season)
▼ PGA & BIGGA
▼ Scottish Golf

**Caddies:**
£50 per caddie per player
(+ gratuity). Book in advance.

**Equipment hire:**
£40 – Titleist and TaylorMade clubs
(includes a sleeve of golf balls)
£25 – electric trolleys

### How do I book a round of golf?

The course is unavailable for play during the winter months, typically between November until mid-March (check course website for details).

There are two ways to book a round of golf at Castle Stuart Golf Links:

*Phone:*
+44 (0) 1463 796111

*Email:*
bookings@castlestuartgolf.com
(include all relevant details – preferred dates/times, group size etc)

### HISTORY

Located just twenty minutes from Loch Ness and Urquhart Castle, the actual castle within the grounds of Castle Stuart Golf Links spent 300 years as a roofless, derelict site before the property was completely renovated.

Mary Queen of Scots gave the castle land to her half-brother, James Stuart, in 1561 along with the title 'Earl of Moray'. James Stuart, 3rd Earl of Moray, finally completed Castle Stuart in 1625. Following the fall of the Stuarts during the conflict with Oliver Cromwell, the castle fell into disrepair. Legend has it the Earl of Moray challenged someone to stay

**View from the 4th tee looking directly towards Castle Stuart.**
*Castle Stuart Golf Links.*

the night in the three-turret bedroom to prove it was not haunted. A local poacher took up the offer and was found dead in the courtyard the next morning...

The golf course opened in the summer of 2009, co-designed by managing partner Mark Parsinen – whose previous developments include Kingsbarns – and course architect Gil Hanse. It was immediately thrust into the spotlight as Golf Magazine voted it 'Best New Course' for 2009. The course has since hosted The Scottish Open in 2011, 2012, 2013 and 2016. Phil Mickelson, victor in 2013, would go on to win The Open Championship a week later at Muirfield.

## PLAYING THE COURSE

The opening three holes on both the front and back-9 run away from the clubhouse and alongside the Moray Firth offering spectacular sea views. The tee-shots from both the 1st and 10th tee (cut into the cliff side above the fairways) offer an exhilarating start for both the out and inward journeys. One clever aspect of the modern design ensures most holes are played in isolation to the rest, with the next hole only revealed once you've finished the current one.

After your opening tee-shot, the first hole is pretty straightforward. Most fairways on the course are quite wide and forgiving. Hole 2 is the first of four par-5s and is reachable in two shots for the big hitters. As you approach the green it appears to be hanging on the edge of the sea, but don't let your eyes play tricks on you as you'll see once you reach it that this is not the case.

**Aerial view of the 3rd hole and the long, narrow green's proximity to the shoreline.**
*Castle Stuart Golf Links.*

**③ SIGNATURE HOLE: PAR-4 3RD, 236–290YDS.**

After a gentle opening get ready for the first test. A solid tee-shot of any description should be able to find the green on this hole. However, there's nothing wrong with taking a safer approach off the tee in favour of a more aggressive approach-shot towards the green. Either way, be sure to avoid the bunkers with your tee-shot and be mindful of the long, narrow green's proximity to the sea.

Hole 4 – the first par-3 – offers a stunning view of the castle directly ahead. There's plenty of room around the green so you can be confident with your tee-shot. The 6th hole is another par-5 with a long and narrow green surrounded by bunkers on the left, right and front. A very testing hole where it would be wiser aiming to get there in three shots.

**The 9th green with the wonderful art deco Clubhouse beyond.** *Castle Stuart Golf Links.*

The 7th is the hardest hole on the course (461yds, par-4). The green stands on the edge of the old sea cliff. The hidden bunkers, while challenging, can save many long approach shots from the abyss beyond. With stunning views of the Chanonry Lighthouse it could be one of the most picturesque settings you'll ever make a bogey on.

After a long par-3 on the 8th, hole 9 brings you back towards the clubhouse with another driveable par-4. However, for those hunting a birdie here, the wiser choice may be hitting to within short-iron territory on the left-hand side of the fairway with the green more visible and receptive from that angle.

The best choice from the 10th tee is to aim for the left of the fairway. Avoid the fairway bunker and the rest is up to you. The 11th hole is a beautiful, short, par-3. Avoid going long at all costs, short and right is the way forward with forgiving contours to putt through the green. Holes 12 through to 15 are testing, but the real fun on the inward part of this course can be found on the final stretch.

The 16th hole is a very driveable par-4, the 17th is a very long par-3 before

**Sunset over the 11th green and Moray Firth.** *Castle Stuart Golf Links.*

the 18th offers up the longest hole on the course. The 16th is begging you to have a go in one so why not? There are a few safety nets left, right and long so what could go wrong? On the 17th (at 224yds this is the longest of all the par-3s) all the danger lies along the right-hand side. A low running shot out to the left is the correct tee-shot with prevailing winds waiting to scoop your ball right if hit too high.

Finally the 18th; 595yds, par-5, with a partially blind tee-shot. For the best line aim directly for the blue Scottish saltire on the left of the clubhouse. It may look daunting for a closing hole, however, be mindful that this hole has the largest green on the course and also offers lots of hidden fairway beyond the sandy area visible in front of the green. A solid approach shot, aimed left, can see you roll up onto the green. A fine finish with a view of the Kessock Bridge beyond.

# 18-hole courses nearby

## ● INVERNESS GOLF CLUB

Established in 1883 this beautiful parkland course received a James Braid redesign and his alterations are still in evidence today. Immaculately kept, the course may not have the length of some of its more famous neighbours in the area but it is a good, solid test for all levels of golfer.

**Website:** www.invernessgolfclub.co.uk
**Email:** manager@invernessgolfclub.co.uk
**Telephone:** +44 (0) 1463 239882

**Par:** 70 (White tees) / 72 (Red tees)
**Length:** 5,528yds–6,026yds
**Type:** Parkland

**Fees:**
▼ per round

## ● FORTROSE & ROSEMARKIE GOLF COURSE

The 15th oldest recorded club in the world also has one of the most breathtakingly scenic courses. Redesigned by James Braid in 1932, his trademarks – tight fairways and strategically placed bunkers – are evident all across the course. On the opposite side of the Moray Firth from Castle Stuart, this course is well worth the short journey over the Kessock Bridge.

**Website:** www.fortrosegolfclub.co.uk
**Email:** secretary@fortrosegolfclub.co.uk
**Telephone:** +44 (0) 1381 620529

**Par:** 71 (White tees) / 71 (Red tees)
**Length:** 5,342yds–5,893yds
**Type:** Links

**Fees:**
▼ per round (weekdays & weekends)

## CRAIL GOLFING SOCIETY – BALCOMIE LINKS

Crail Golfing Society,
Crail,
Fife,
KY10 3XN
**www.crailgolfingsociety.co.uk**
**Phone:** +44 (0) 1333 450686
**Email:** info@crailgolfingsociety.co.uk

---

**Essential course details –**

**Par:** 69 (White tees) / 72 (Red tees)

**S.S.S:** 70

**Slope:** 122 (White tees) / 120 (Red tees)

**Length:** 5,207yds–5,861yds

**Longest hole:** Par-5 12th, 514yds–525yds

**Shortest hole:** Par-3 14th, 132yds–147yds

**Type:** Links

---

**Handicap Certificate:** Not required.

**Green fees:**
▼ per round
▼ full day ticket (one round each Balcomie / Craighead)

Reduced green fee rates typically apply 1 October–31 December.

**Caddies:**
£50 per golfer per round (+ gratuity). Must be booked in advance.

**Equipment Hire:**
£40 – buggy

£35 – golf clubs
£15 – power trolley
£6 – push trolley
£5 – pull trolley

### How do I book a round of golf?

Crail Golfing Society is a private members club, however, it welcomes visitors at all times during the week for both the Balcomie and Craighead links courses.

There are three ways to book a round of golf at Crail Golfing Society – Balcomie Links Course.

*Online:*
Make a booking via the online booking system on the official website – www.crailgolfingsociety.co.uk/PublicBook/

*Phone:*
+44 (0) 1333 450686

*Email:*
info@crailgolfingsociety.co.uk (include all relevant details – preferred dates/times, group size etc)

---

### HISTORY

Crail is the oldest borough in Fife and was a thriving port for many years during the middle ages. It was here Mary of Guise, mother of Mary Queen of Scots, landed in 1538 en

Back of the 13th green looking down towards the 14th green and rugged coastline along the right side of the course. *Crail Golfing Society.*

route to her marriage to James V at St Andrews.

Crail Golfing Society, reputedly the seventh oldest golf club in the world, was formally created on 23 February 1786 with an inaugural meeting of eleven members at the Golf Inn in Crail:

> Several gentlemen in and about the Town of Crail who were fond of the diversion of golf agreed to form themselves into a Society which should be known by the name of the Crail Golfing Society.

> (Source: www.scottishgolfhistory.org)

The original club links were at Sauchope just up the coast from Crail and was a nine-hole course. The site is now a caravan park. The club would struggle in its infancy and it was not until the late nineteenth century, with the rise of the railway and industrial revolution, that Crail became caught up in the new golfing boom of the time.

In 1895 Crail left Sauchope to play at Balcomie Links – at the time another 9-hole course laid down by Old Tom Morris in 1892. Old Tom would return in 1896 to add another nine.

## PLAYING THE COURSE

As golf continues to bulldoze its way through the 'age of the big hitters' it would be very easy to look at Balcomie Links total yardage and feel that the course must be a soft touch. This would be a very unwise assumption. Shots over rocky bays, long par-3s with greens perched on top of vertical cliffs, shots to greens seemingly engulfed by gorse, curving par fours round sandy strands – daring the golfer to cut off too much, shots from cliff tops to greens and fairways invitingly laid out below. These are just a few of the challenges that await you as you stand on the first tee at Balcomie. Old Mr Morris knew a thing or two about how to test every facet of a golfer's game.

The first thing to note is the rich variety of holes here – three par-5s, six par-3s and nine par-4s combine for a tough overall par score of 69 from the white tees and 72 from the red tees. The wind, as with so many of its links cousins along the coast, can be a major factor. As the official website states, the greens are always maintained at a speed of between 7 and 9 on the stimpmeter – any faster and they become unplayable in high winds.

The first ten holes at Balcomie Links are quite unique in a way that might not be good news for any of us prone to the odd right-hand slice. Anything too far over to starboard will see your ball either in the sea or in the middle of farmland. Either way it's out of bounds.

The same advice is given to all visitors who play Balcomie Links for the first time in reference to these opening holes: 'You have the whole of Scotland on your left-hand side. So, keep it left.'

The first hole sets the tone for the round with an opening drive from the cliff top down onto the fairway. The left-hand side gives you the best angle into a large green. Be sure to avoid the large front bunker with your approach.

Hole 2 is the first of three par-5s and with the North Sea running along the right-hand side your drive needs to aim left with a blind second shot straight over the mound leaving a chip on to the green. Not a long par-5, just don't aim right. Hole 3 – the first par-3 rewards accuracy – drifting in from the left is the best option.

> **5 SIGNATURE HOLE: PAR-4 5TH, 427–447YDS – 'HELL'S HOLE'.**
> Ryder Cup Captain, Sam Torrance gave his approval to the name of this hole and believes it to be the hardest par-4 in Scotland. The classic risk and reward dilemma – how much of the coastline are you prepared to slice off to get closer to the green? Pick a spot and commit to it.

The remaining front nine culminates with a short par-4 at the 9th hole with supreme bunker protection for those attempting to drive up to the green. Aim for the large bunker at the front but make sure to land short, leaving a short iron approach on to the putting surface.

Holes 11 and 12 are back-to-back par-5s offering lots of space from the tee so don't hold back. The 12th is a genuine 3-shot par-5. Best to lay up before the burn with the 2nd shot before a tricky 3rd on to a heavily contoured green.

**7th green perfectly illustrating the close proximity of the shoreline to the course.** *Crail Golfing Society.*

After back-to-back par-5s you're then faced with back-to-back par-3s. Hole 13 is a long par-3 playing uphill leaving a semi-blind shot off the tee on to an undulating green. A bogey here should not be frowned upon – take it and scarper. Hole 14, the shortest on the course, is a favourite among many club members. Your tee-shot is taken from the top of the cliffs, next to the

**The shared 8th and 11th green with the Clubhouse and pro-shop atop the cliffs in the background.** *Crail Golfing Society.*

clubhouse, down toward a large, inviting green with the beach to your right and the old boathouse right behind. Don't get too caught up with the fantastic vantage point from the tee. A good, accurate shot is still required.

The next four holes – two par-3s and two par-4s – all require focus on club selection where, if in doubt, take an extra club length. Unusually for a final hole, the round closes with a par-3 18th. So, take in the view one last time before setting up for a long tee-shot. Aim left of the green for the best area to fade towards the hole.

# Other courses on site

In addition to the Balcomie Links course, Crail Golfing Society also has the following course available for visitors to play:

### ● CRAIGHEAD LINKS (18 HOLES)

Opened in 1998, Craighead Links was the first course outside of the USA designed by renowned architect, Gil Hanse. With no two consecutive holes facing in the same direction and with no tress lining the fairway, this is a true test of traditional golf links where managing the wind is an integral part of playing the course.

Sat on top of a cliff, the views are simply stunning and the sea is visible from every hole. The course offers four different tees with lengths ranging from 5,340–6,651yds and par scores from 69 (blue tees), 72 (yellow and white tees) and 74 (red).

Booking a round for Craighead Links follows the exact same route and options as detailed above for Balcomie Links. The combined day ticket is a perfect way to compare and contrast both courses.

**Par:** 72 (White tees) / 74 (Red tees)
**Length:** 5,340–6,651yds

**Green fees:**
▼ per round

Reduced green fee rates typically apply 1 October–31 December.

**5**

## CRUDEN BAY GOLF CLUB – CHAMPIONSHIP COURSE

Cruden Bay Golf Club,
Aulton Road,
Cruden Bay,
Aberdeenshire,
Scotland,
AB42 0NN
**www.crudenbaygolfclub.co.uk**
**Phone:** +44 (0) 1779 812285
**Email:** bookings@crudenbaygolfclub.
co.uk

Essential course details –
**Par:** 70 (White tees) / 73 (Red tees)
**S.S.S:** 71 (White tees) / 74 (Red tees)
**Slope rating:** 125 (White) / 138 (Red)
**Length:** 5,724yds–6,263yds
**Longest hole:** par-5 13th, 487yds–571yds
**Shortest hole:** par-3 11th, 138yds–150yds
Type: Links

**Handicap Certificate:** Not required

**Green fees:**
▼ * per adult per round (Weekdays & Weekends**)
▼ * under-18s per round
▼ 36 holes per Adult
▼ 36 holes under-18s

* = Includes 9 holes at St Olaf Course on the same day, time permitting.
**= Weekends, main course available 'pm' only.

**Caddies:**
£50 per player per round (+gratuity) (book in advance)

**Equipment hire:**
£35 – club hire
£15 – electric trolley
£5 – pull trolley

There are no buggies available due to the terrain.

**How do I book a round of golf?**
Cruden Bay Golf Club is a private members club however visitors are welcome to play seven days a week subject to availability. On weekends tee-times are available after 2 pm on Saturday and after 12.30 pm on Sunday.

There are two ways to book a round of golf for the Championship Course at Cruden Bay:

*Phone:*
+44(0) 1779 812285

*Email:*
elaine@crudenbaygolfclub.co.uk
(include all relevant details – preferred dates/times, group size etc)

## HISTORY
There is evidence, in the form of a ballot box inscribed 'Cruden Golf Club 1791', that a nine-hole golf course existed before the current

The sunsets over Cruden Bay, underneath the Starter's Hut, with Slains Castle in the distance. *Cruden Bay Golf Club.*

layout. The course, as we know it now, was commissioned in 1894 by the Great North of Scotland Railway Company and fully opened in 1899 as part of the recreational facilities offered by the newly erected Cruden Bay Hotel, opened in March of that same year.

Originally designed by Old Tom Morris, with help from Archie Simpson, the Championship Course opening was celebrated with an inaugural professional two-day open tournament on 14-15 April 1899. Harry Vardon, James Braid and Ben Sayers were all among the field with prizes totalling £120. It would be Vardon who emerged as the eventual winner.

The Cruden Bay Golf Club was formed around 1900, the first Captain being the Reverend B Alcock. In 1926 Tom Simpson and Herbert Fowler redesigned the course to the current layout. They also redesigned the St Olaf course, which was opened at the same time. The structure now used as the Starters Hut is actually the original Clubhouse.

Visible from most parts of the course is the imposing ruin of New Slains Castle – supposedly an influence for Bram Stoker; the author holidayed in Cruden Bay when writing Dracula.

## PLAYING THE COURSE

Looking out over the links from the elevated clubhouse, the dune land here looks as though it was heaven made for golf. Cruden Bay is a rugged and natural links where the golfing test has remained consistent for the past one hundred years. An extremely picturesque and peaceful location, the real world seems rather distant. This is golfing escapism at its best.

As you stand on the first tee and assess the stunning panorama you could be forgiven for thinking your driver may not see much action during this round. With some truly monumental dunes, covered in thick rough and surrounding the course, placement is definitely the key word here. You'll enjoy yourself a lot more if you play smart rather than bold.

The first three holes are all par-4s of varying lengths and difficulty. Hole 1 is fairly routine allowing you to open your shoulders from the tee and really swing through the ball. The 2nd sits on top of a mound with a steep slope off the front making any approach shot quite perilous and difficult for the ball to hold its position. The short 3rd is more troublesome than it looks from the yardage (367 yards from the blue tees, 268 yards from the whites) as bumps and borrows of every description sit in front of a green that lies below the level of the fairway.

Most courses ease you in during the first five or six holes but not here. At Cruden Bay your honeymoon ends at the 3rd hole. The 4th, 5th, 6th and 7th are where the course starts to come alive and show its teeth as you're faced with rising dunes and water hazards.

The wind has a lot to do with this. The first 3 holes usually play with the wind behind you, holes 4 through to 10 play with the wind in front of you.

**The view from the tee at the 4th hole, the green laid out in front and Port Erroll Harbour on your left.** *Cruden Bay Golf Club.*

**4** **SIGNATURE HOLE: PAR-3 4TH, 142–196YDS.**
The tee for this hole has the village behind you with the river on the left leading to Port Erroll harbour and the hole sitting above you directly in front. It's without doubt one of the prettiest holes you could ever drop shots on. And drop them you will if you don't choose the right club, as this hole is all carry up to the green. In fact, take one club more than you need even if that club is a driver. Miss the green and a dropped shot or shots are nigh on a certainty.

**One of the most awe-inspiring views you'll find on any golf course – the 9th tee at Cruden Bay's Championship Course.** *Cruden Bay Golf Club.*

The very driveable par-4 8th offers some relief between the previous four holes and the newly designed 9th. Previously seen as the most ordinary hole on the course, the 9th could now lay claim to be among the finest. A steep climb up to the tee reveals the most incredible vista across the bay. It's hard to imagine another golf course offering a more breathtaking spectacle than what you see from here. The fairway has a slight dogleg right running alongside the cliff up to the green perched on the edge offering more spectacular views.

The 10th hole is another elevated tee-shot, which can play a few mind games with you. Aim more left than you feel you need to from the tee over the banking. You're hitting down towards the fairway where two bunkers await anything too far left. If you're unsure, grab a crafty look as you walk from the 9th green. The green sits under the shadow of the cliffs with two bunkers at the front and one on the left, leaving a tricky approach shot.

After the routine 12th hole, the next set of holes are possibly the most challenging on the course. The 13th sets you up for a blind approach shot to a green built into the side of the cliff below the 9th hole. The 14th takes you alongside the beach and up to one of the most famous greens in Scotland – 'the bathtub'. Hole 15 is a long par-3 blind tee-shot over a large sand dune with only a marker post to guide you. Don't forget to ring the bell when you're done on the green to let any group behind you know they're free to take their tee-shots.

Hole 16 is another challenging par-3 before you close out your round with two medium-length par-4s. The 17th requires a precise approach shot towards an elevated green. Two bunkers front-left and one front-right protects the front, while a steep slope toward thick gorse protects the back. The 18th is a split-level fairway bending to the right with one bunker protecting the front-right of the green.

Pin flag colours on the course represent where the hole sits on the green. Red means front of the green, yellow – middle and blue means at the back.

# Other courses on site

In addition to the championship course, Cruden Bay Golf Club also has the following course available for visitors to play:

### ● ST OLAF (9 HOLES)

As you approach Cruden Bay Golf Club from the main road, most of the holes you see are actually part of the St Olaf course rather than the championship course. With four par-3s and five par-4s, St Olaf is a highly regarded links test in its own right. When you travel to Cruden Bay be sure to leave time for a go on both these wonderful courses.

**Par:** 32 (Blue tees) / 34 (Red tees)
**S.S.S:** 32 (Blue tees) / 34 (Red tees)
**Length:** 2,355yds–2,433yds

**Green fees:**
▼ 9-holes (weekdays & weekends)
▼ 18-holes (weekdays & weekends)
(9-hole price guide)

# 18-hole courses nearby

### ● PETERHEAD GOLF CLUB – OLD COURSE

Set among the glorious Craigewan links, another fine example of golf along rugged coastline. Designed by Willie Park Jnr in 1892, originally as a 9-hole course, extended to 18 holes in 1908. There's also a 9-hole course called, appropriately, the New Course.

**Website:** www.peterheadgolfclub.co.uk
**Email:** enquiries@peterheadgolfclub.co.uk
**Telephone:** +44 (0) 1779 472149

**Par:** 70 (White tees) / 72 (Red tees)
**Length:** 5,382yds–6,147yds
**Type:** Links

**Fees:**
Orange: per round (weekday & weekend)

### ● FRASERBURGH GOLF CLUB – CORBIE HILL

Redesigned by James Braid, you have everything you need for a truly invigorating links challenge. There's also a 9-hole course called Rosehill.

**Website:** www.fraserburghgolf.club
**Email:** secretary@ fraserburghgolfclub.org
**Telephone:** +44 (0) 1346 516616

**Par:** 70 (White tees) / 74 (Red tees)
Length: 5,323yds–6,308yds
**Type:** Links

**Fees:**
▼ per round (weekday & weekend)

### ● INVERALLOCHY GOLF CLUB

Founded in 1888, surrounded by unspoilt, natural beauty. The course is quite short by modern standards due mainly to having six par-3s, but is still a test for all golfers – particularly when the wind is blowing.

**Website:** www.inverallochygolfclub.com
**Telephone:** +44 (0) 1346 582000

**Par:** 67 (White tees) / 66 (Yellow tees)
**Length:** 5,066yds-5,436yds
**Type:** Links

**Fees:**
▼ per round (weekday & weekend)

# DUNDONALD LINKS

Dundonald Links,
Ayr Road,
Gailes,
Ayrshire, KA11 5BF
**www.dundonaldlinks.com**
**Phone:** +44 (0) 1294 314000
**Email:** reservations@dundonaldlinks.com

**Essential course details –**
**Par:** 72 (All tees)
**S.S.S:** 76 (Black tees) / 73 (Red tees)
**Slope rating:** 138 (Black tees) /
131 (Red tees)
**Length:** 5,560yds–7,100yds
**Longest hole:** Par-5 18th, 480yds–560yds
**Shortest hole:** Par-3 11th, 100yds–120yds
**Type:** Links

**Handicap Certificate:** Not required

**Green fees:**
▼ per round

**Caddies:**
£50 per person per round (+ gratuity).

**Equipment hire:**
Clubs, buggies and trollies available
upon request – book in advance via
reservations email or telephone.

**How do I book a round of golf?**
There are three ways to book a round
of golf at Dundonald Links:

*Online:*
Make a booking via the online
booking system on the official
website – www.dundonaldlinks.com/
bookings

*Phone:*
+44 (0) 1294 314000

*Email:*
Reservations@dundonaldlinks.
com (include all relevant details –
preferred dates/times, group size etc)

## HISTORY

With such esteemed neighbours
along the Ayrshire coast as Royal
Troon and Prestwick you'd be forgiven
for thinking Dundonald Links also
originated from the same golden
era of course design – but you'd be
wrong. Opened in 2003 and, in a very
short space of time, the course has
already gained a solid reputation as a
classic modern links.

Many decades ago the site
originally housed Dundonald Golf
Club but it fell into disrepair and was
converted for military use during
the Second World War, where troops
practiced the famous D-Day Landings,
eventually returning to wasteland.

At the turn of the millennium a
new course was conceived by revered
businessman, Yaqub Ali, to be known

as Southern Gailes. The site was the original home to Fort Donald, which in Gaelic, translates as Dundonald thus a swift change of names was put forward – Dundonald Links. Yaqub envisioned a course that could be used by everyone in the area, not just a privileged few.

Unfortunately, Yaqub would lose a long battle with cancer before seeing his project reach completion. Yaqub entrusted acclaimed architect, Kyle Phillips as course designer to realise his dream. Along with the new site owners, Loch Lomond Golf Club, Kyle finished the course with its first day of play taking place on the 1 July 2003.

As early as 2008, the course was chosen as the venue for the first stage of the European Tour Qualifying School. In 2012, it played host to the Senior Open Qualifying. The course then hosted the Ladies Scottish Open in 2015, 2016 and 2017. Most recently Dundonald heralded the arrival of the Men's Scottish Open in 2017.

## PLAYING THE COURSE

The defining feature of Dundonald Links is without doubt the wide fairways, becoming narrower as you approach the greens – a classic trait of a Kyle Phillips design. The increase in difficulty as you approach the pin creates a different links test, rather than wading through long grass or thick gorse looking for your ball, club selection and accuracy in your approach shot become key.

The first hole, 430yds par-4, would appear to be fairly straight and gentle but don't be fooled. There's a fairway bunker on the left waiting for your tee-shot, the green is well guarded on both sides with a slope back to front and a hollow on the front right. A par is a very good start.

After a par-4 dogleg right 2nd hole, you move onto the opening par-5, the first of four on the course. Accuracy is required from the tee if you're to avoid the ditch spanning the fairway from right to left. The smart play is to lay up near the fairway bunker. Approach shots need to be wary of the bunker front-right and one spanning the back of the green waiting to catch any long balls.

Next comes the first par-3 and at 195yds from the blue tee playing into the wind, it's a long one. Aim front-right to avoid the bunkers left and right. There's also trouble at the back so coming up slightly short is not a disaster as there's plenty of scope to putt onto the green.

Holes 7 and 8 are two stunning par-4s with the Isle of Arran as a backdrop. The front nine comes to a close with another, tricky, par-4. The 9th green is

The undulating green at the par-3 11th with Ailsa Craig on the horizon.
*Mark Alexander Golf Photography.*

**11** **SIGNATURE HOLE: PAR-3 11TH, 100–120YDS.**
The fun on the back-9 starts at the par-3 11th. Three deep bunkers guard the left of the green so aim towards the right and watch the ball gather towards the centre. If you're too long you could end up in a bunker called the 'cauldron', a remnant from the original course discovered, and subsequently retained, by Kyle Phillips during its redevelopment.

well protected by a ditch running across the front and two pot bunkers. If your approach requires a long iron or wood, it may be worth going for the green in three and avoiding any disasters.

The 12th is the shortest par-4 at 335yds from the blue tees with stunning views of the Firth of Clyde. Three hidden pot bunkers and a left to right prevailing cross-wind all mean the approach shot needs to be well controlled.

A links course isn't complete without a hole near a railway line and at

**Sunset over the 12th fairway looking towards the green.** *Mark Alexander Golf Photography.*

**Looking back down the 14th fairway towards the railway line in the far-left corner.**
*Mark Alexander Golf Photography.*

Dundonald Links you'll find it running alongside the 13th. A straight drive is essential to set up for a tricky approach shot that needs to get over a ditch at the front of the two-tiered green.

The 15th is a long par-3 that plays every inch of its yardage. The best spot is somewhere on the right side of the green to avoid two bunkers protecting the front left section. Hole 16, a 450yds par-4, is the toughest hole on the course. Avoid the fairway bunkers to leave a long approach shot into a two-tier green. There's no shame in 'laying up' to pitch onto the green. A bogey should feel like a par and is a good score at this hole.

The longest hole on the course is saved for the par-5 18th. The shape and positioning of the fairway bunkers make it almost certain three solid shots are needed to reach the green. Aim left from the tee to avoid trouble, an accurate second is needed but with a ditch guarding the front of the green there's huge risks in trying to get there without a short pitch onto the putting surface. Don't try and be a hero right at the end, be smart and avoid any card spoilers.

# 18-hole courses nearby

## ● KILMARNOCK (BARASSIE) GOLF CLUB – BARASSIE LINKS

Offering a championship layout with an interesting mixture of old style links and a more modern layout. The course is essentially split into two sets of nine – one from the original course dating back to the late eighteenth century and one set built in 1997. With 27 holes at the course there are actually three different 18-hole configurations to choose from. The Barassie layout is the longest of the three.

**Website:** www.kbgc.co.uk
**Email:** gm@kbgc.co.uk
**Telephone:** +44 (0) 1292 313920

**Par:** 72 (White tees) / 75 (Red tees)
Length: 6,094yds–6,852yds
Type: Links

**Fees:**
▼ per round (weekday & weekend)

## GLENEAGLES – THE KING'S COURSE

The Gleneagles Hotel,
Auchterarder,
Perthshire,
PH3 1NF
**www.gleneagles.com**
**Phone:** +44 (0) 1764 662231 / USA: 1 866 881 9525 (Toll Free)
**Email:** Gleneagles.golf@gleneagles.com

Essential course details –
**Par:** 68 (Yellow tees) / 71 (Red tees)
**S.S.S:** 71 (Yellow & Red tees)
**Slope rating:** 126 (Yellow tees) / 129 (Red tees)
**Length:** 5,211yds–6,057yds
**Longest hole:** Par-4 6th, 391yds–455yds
**Shortest hole:** Par-3 16th, 113yds–128yds
**Type:** Inland

**Handicap Certificate:** Not required

**Green fees:**
▼ Hotel guest & visitor (low season)
▼ Hotel guest (shoulder season)
▼ Visitor (shoulder season)
▼ Hotel guest (high season)
▽ Visitor (high season)
▼ Juniors (17 years and under)

**Caddies:**
£60 per player per round. Group Caddie available – £23.75 per player, three-player minimum.

**Equipment hire:**
£57.50 – clubs (includes trolley and 3 golf balls) / £42.50 (exc. trolley and balls)
£8 – trolley
£25 – shoes

### How do I book a round of golf?
There are three ways to book a round of golf for The King's Course at Gleneagles:

*Online:*
Via main website – www.gleneagles.com

*Phone:*
+44 (0) 1764 662231
USA: 1 866 881 9525 (Toll Free)

*Email:*
Gleneagles.golf@gleneagles.com
OR resort.sales@gleneagles.com
(include all relevant details – preferred dates/times, group size etc.)

### HISTORY
Taking time out from his busy role as General Manager of the Caledonian Railway Company in 1910, Donald Matheson convalesced among the stunning beauty of the Scottish Highlands. Inspired by this natural,

**Looking down the 9th fairway towards the green at the King's Course.** *Gleneagles.*

awe-inspiring atmosphere he began to formulate plans for a Grand Hotel surrounded by three golf courses.

Fourteen years later – delayed as a result of the outbreak of the Great War – this grand idea would be realised in the form of The Gleneagles Hotel. Two of the courses would be opened long before the hotel. First, The King's Course on 1 May 1919 followed by The Queen's Course – initially a 9-hole course before being redeveloped into 18 holes in 1925. Five-times Open Champion and a member of the Great Triumvirate, James Braid, designed both courses.

In 1921, a practice match was arranged between twelve US golfers and twelve British (including Braid). The idea being the American golfers could do with as much practice as possible ahead of The Open Championship as no US golfer had emerged victorious at that time.

The matchplay format (eventually becoming 10 v 10 due to dropouts) took place at The King's Course on 6 June with the British emerging victorious by nine matches to three and three matches drawn. Jock Hutchison, a member of the defeated US team, would go on to become the first US-based winner* of

---

* = Hutchison was actually born in St Andrews, Scotland and moved to America in 1900 before becoming a US citizen in 1920. Walter Hagen became the first native-born American to win The Open a year later in 1922.

the claret jug at St Andrews a few weeks later, thus, the original objective set out by the USGA was achieved.

No further corresponding fixtures were arranged until 1926, however, the match at Gleneagles was the foundation for what would become known as The Ryder Cup.

## PLAYING THE COURSE

Regarded by many as the finest inland course Scotland has to offer, recent modifications ahead of its centenary have seen The King's Course layout returned to the one first envisioned by its architect, James Braid. The work reversed a lot of changes made in the late 80s, increasing fairway width by around 40 per cent, therefore, bringing a number of bunkers back in from the rough. These changes have given 'The King's' much more of an Inland Links feel, possessing fast-running fairways with cut-lines down to 8mm.

Upon first sight The King's Course appears carved through the pine trees as it rises and falls over springy moorland turf. It may not be the longest, but with blind shots, humps, hollows and testing greens, this is a course that will only reward precise and considered play.

There are five different tee-boxes to choose from which can alter the overall par-score. Be sure and check with the starter as to which tee-box they would recommend based on your ability.

Accuracy from the tee is essential here. The first four holes all appear very manageable, short par-4s, but don't be fooled – from first glance they appear much shorter than they actually are, so keep checking the distances on your scorecard against what your eyes are telling you and take care with your club choice.

The 1st hole is a fairly straightforward par-4. Aim your tee-shot towards the right of the fairway to leave yourself the best line in with your approach to an elevated green protected by four bunkers, especially a particularly large one right at the front.

The King's Course is well known for the relatively high number of 'saddles' on the fairways. Around twelve holes offer tee-shots where you play over a rise in the land on the fairway and can't see the landing area you're aiming for. The 3rd hole, for example, requires a solid iron or 3-wood off the tee with a completely blind second over what seems like a 'mountain' to a large two-tiered green, with a very steep slope between tiers, beyond.

The 6th hole plays as either a par-5 or par-4 depending on the tee and offers a further test with a signature saddle to aim over with your drive. Try to avoid going too far left to leave yourself with an approach which can fall just short of the green as the ball will run forward from the front.

**Stunning backdrop behind the 17th green, King's Course.**
*Gleneagles.*

If the wind is in play (bear in mind you're in the highlands so better to expect it than not), then you'll feel it most into your face from the 3rd hole through to the 8th. It's only once you've turned back towards home that you will feel more in control with the wind behind.

The wonderful par-4 12th is called 'Tappit Hen' and refers to the group of trees on a hill behind the green – the highest point on the course. Another blind tee-shot that you should try and keep left. This will leave the best approach into a green with all the bunker protection toward the front so you can be bullish here to avoid landing short.

Holes 16, 17 and 18 offer a thrilling finale to your round where every bump and hump can come into play. The 16th is the shortest hole but can play very tough with a green surrounded by bunkers and a steep ridge off the back. Hole 17 has the tightest fairway on the course so be accurate with your drive.

At the end of the round you're left with a feeling of having played golf within its most natural habitat. No modern-day course layout can come close to replicating such a terrain, after all, how do you duplicate a mountain?

**18** ) **SIGNATURE HOLE: PAR-4/5 18TH, 'KING'S HAME'.**
The 18th plays as either a par-4 or a comfortable par-5, depending on which colour tee you play from, with the largest green on the course that can create a two-club difference between front and back. Be mindful of where the pin is when making your club choice for your last approach.

# Other courses on site

In addition to The King's Course, Gleneagles also has the following courses available for visitors to play:

### ● THE QUEEN'S COURSE (18 HOLES)

Opened just after The King's, The Queen's Course also has a fabulous setting threading through the north and west sides of the Gleneagles estate. 'The Queen's' has also received some recent modifications with a number of trees both removed and added in certain places with the encouragement of heather to give this course much more of a heathland feel to the overall layout.

Don't be fooled by the natural beauty on show as this course, despite being shorter than The King's, will still challenge all facets of your game. The first six holes are as hard a start to a course as you'll find anywhere in Scotland.

**Par:** 68 (White tees) / 74 (Red tees)
**S.S.S:** 69 (White tees) / 72 (Red tees)

**Slope rating:** 121 (White tees) / 131 (Red tees)
**Length:** 5,495yds–5,965yds

**Green fees:**
▼ Hotel guest & visitor (low season)
▼ Hotel guest (shoulder season)
▼ Visitor (shoulder season)
▼ Hotel guest (high season)
▼ Visitor (high season)
▼ Juniors (17 years and under)

### ● THE PGA CENTENARY COURSE (18 HOLES)

Venue for the 2014 Ryder Cup which saw Paul McGinley's European team cruise to victory by five points against a strong USA team. Since hosting The Ryder Cup, this course has been made much more playable with thinned out rough and fairways allowing for the ball to sit up

**Deep bunker hiding at the back of the 9th green, Queen's Course.**
*Gleneagles.*

Incredible vista surrounds the 18th green, PGA Centenary Course. *Gleneagles.*

(typical cut heights are 15mm) which, in turn, caters for more height through the air creating a modern classic feel.

**Par:** 72 (White tees) / 71 (Red tees)
**S.S.S:** 74 (White tees) / 71 (Red tees)
**Slope rating:** 141 (White tees) / 128 (Red tees)
**Length:** 5,271yds–6,804yds

**Green fees:**
▼ Hotel guest & visitor (low season)
▼ Hotel guest (shoulder season)
▼ Visitor (shoulder season)
▼ Hotel guest (high season)
▼ Visitor (high season)
▼ Juniors (17 years and under)

### ● THE PGA NATIONAL ACADEMY COURSE (9 HOLES)

Evolved from the originally named 'Wee course', which was built and designed in 1928 by Head Greenkeeper, George Alexander. A great testing ground to hone your skills before heading out on to the bigger courses on the estate.

**Par:** 27
**Length:** 1,431yds

**Green fees:**
▼ Hotel guest and visitors per round (low to high season)
(9-hole price guide)

# 18-hole courses nearby

### ● NORTH INCH GOLF COURSE

Around 18 miles along the A9 you'll find the home of the Royal Perth Golfing Society; the first Golf Club in the world to have been bestowed the 'Royal' title in 1833, one year before the Royal and Ancient Golf Club of St Andrews. A lovely, historic parkland course set right in the heart of Perth.

**Website:** www.northinchgolf.co.uk
**Email:** northinchgolf@pkc.gov.uk
**Telephone:** +44 (0) 1738 636481

**Par:** 68
**Length:** 5,442yds

**Type:** Parkland

**Fees:**
▼ per round (weekdays and weekends)

**8**

## GOLF HOUSE CLUB, ELIE – LINKS COURSE

The Golf House Club,
Elie,
Fife,
Scotland,
KY9 1AS
www.golfhouseclub.co.uk
Phone: + 44 (0) 1333 330301
Email: book@golfhouseclub.org

### Essential course details –

**Par:** 70 (White tees) / 73 (Red tees)

**S.S.S:** 70 (White tees) / 73 (Red tees)

**Slope rating:** Not available

**Length:** 5,768yds–6,273yds

**Longest hole:** par-4 12th, 415yds–466yds

**Shortest hole:** par-3 11th, 131yds

**Type:** Links

**Handicap Certificate:** Required (Maximum permitted – 28 for men and 36 for ladies)

**Green fees:**
▼ adult per round (weekday)
▼ adult per round (weekend)
▼ junior per round (weekday & weekend)

**Caddies:**
£50 (+gratuity).

**Equipment hire:**
Clubs, buggies and push trolleys

are all available upon request. It is recommended to reserve a buggy at the same time as booking your round.

### How do I book a round of golf?

The Golf House Club, Elie, is a private members club but welcomes visitors at all times during the week. Visitors are able to book tee-times usually after 10.30 am each day unless there is a competition taking place.

There are three ways to book a round of golf at The Golf House Club – Links Course.

*Online:*
www.golfhouseclub.co.uk/visitor-information/tee-time-availability-booking/

*Phone:*
+44 (0) 1333 330301

*Email:*
book@golfhouseclub.org (include all relevant details – preferred dates/times, group size etc)

### HISTORY

The beautiful villages of Earlsferry and Elie have, for centuries, been bound together by their cherished links course. Around the same time as Columbus was discovering the Americas and battles raged to prove

**Deep bunkers surround the 2nd green. The highest point on the course offers stunning views of the Firth of Forth and East Lothian beyond.** *Golf House Club, Elie.*

the earth was not actually flat, a Royal Charter confirmed that golf was played over the 'golfing tract' in Earlsferry.

Such documents, therefore, suggest the golf links to be among the oldest courses in the world. However, it would not be until 1770 that mention would be made of a formal course layout. Two to be precise – both a short course and a long course are confirmed in official documents from the time. As with a number of its counterparts, the Elie Links Course would face protest from local farmers who saw it as prized agricultural land going to waste on a leisure activity.

The first hard evidence of golfing activity on the site comes from an entry in the Caledonian Mercury dated 1 May 1787, announcing a dinner to be held for the Earlsferry Golf Society. All members were expected to attend with dinner on the table at three o' clock.

A twenty-year dispute between the course dwellers and a local landowner would be settled following legal action in 1832 securing the rights of the golfers to use the land. The Earlsferry and Elie Golf Club was formed in 1858, however the two village entities would eventually split in 1912. The Elie members continued to play on the original links and purchased more land to extend the course and build a clubhouse.

The burgh of Elie & Earlsferry was also a prominent base for some of the most revered golf club makers in the land. One of the foremost among his peers was Andrew Herd Scott (1875–1934). Upon the coronation of George V in 1911, Scott was appointed club maker to the king. Previously, Scott was club maker to HRH the Prince of Wales.

The Golf House Club came into existence in 1875, taking its name from the clubhouse, which was completed two years later. More land was acquired in 1886 and 1896, leading to final expansion and a full 18-hole course. Today's layout is said to be very similar to the original design completed at this time.

In 1974 The Golf House Club was able to purchase the land on which the course lies securing its future for generations to come.

## PLAYING THE COURSE

At 6,273yds Elie is, by no means, a long course. It has no par-5s at all and only two par-3s, leaving 16 par-4s ranging from 284yds to 466yds. However, Elie is not a course that gives up good scores easily and is a true links terrain combining undulating fairways with large, fast and firm greens.

Elie requires patience – you need to craft your way round this course rather than blast your way round. A layout that will make you think before you swing. A network of bunkers are strategically placed to catch anything that strays offline or distance is misjudged. The fast, contoured greens add another layer of protection and are regarded as being among the best in the country.

As you stand on the 1st tee you will notice two things that make a round at Elie such a unique experience. The first and most salient feature is the periscope, which towers 10 metres above the starters hut. Rescued from HMS *Excalibur* in 1966, visitors are encouraged to take a look before they start their round and appreciate the incredible 360-degree views it provides.

The second feature(s) are the unusual tee-boxes. Invented and patented in 1907 by David West, an artist and scratch golfer from Lossiemouth. Because of the unusual design with rests for golf bags they were christened 'Tee Caddies'. The only other course to have them is Moray Golf Club where West was a regular.

The par-4 1st hole throws you straight into the action with a blind tee-shot over the brow of a hill. Hit it too far right and you may be out of bounds or in a bunker. The large green will also test your putting skills from the start. Hole 2 is called 'High Hole' as it's the highest point on the course offering stunning views across the Firth of Forth to Muirfield and North Berwick. At 284yds it is driveable, however with the green surrounded by bunkers the safe shot is to lay up and go at the green with a short iron. There is a steep run off at the back of the green so accuracy is crucial.

The first of two par-3s comes next and at 214yds, depending on the strength

The unique site of the periscope above the Starter's Hut greets you on the first tee. *Golf House Club, Elie.*

of the wind, the tee-shot may be anything from a mid-iron to a driver. Anything short will be mopped up by well-placed bunkers both right and left and out of bounds at the back.

The remaining front-9 holes are all par-4 of varying difficulty. Most will tempt you with a driver off the tee but beware of the bunker positions and go with a long iron if you're unsure of hitting over them. The pick of the bunch is hole 8, the most difficult on the course. With thick rough running down the left and a red path running across at a right angle, this gives the impression of a narrowing fairway. Playing towards the left corner should offer the better approach shot onto the green, protected by a deep bunker at the front-right.

Hole 11 is the second par-3 and is called 'Sea Hole' as it stands at the waters edge. At only 131 yards a careful short iron needs to be played just right of centre in order to roll into the middle of the green.

**(13) SIGNATURE HOLE: PAR-4 13TH, 355–380YDS, 'CROUPIE'.**
Elie local, James Braid, knew a thing or two about golf courses and he called this hole the finest in the country. A drive towards the right of centre leaves you with the best angle towards the green. The approach into the hole is another signature shot, as it needs to carry all the way over a deep hollow that lies in front of the green.

**Rugged landscape and the shoreline surround the 12th and 13th fairways.** *Golf House Club, Elie.*

The remaining back-9 are all par-4s leading up to the 18th that is conveniently called 'Home'. As you hit for home, the tee-shot here needs to be solid and straight to avoid the bunkers both left and right. The green is protected by two more that sit 50yds from the front. Nothing too big or too short will do for the approach onto this green – right in the centre will do just fine.

# 18-hole courses nearby

### ● LUNDIN GOLF CLUB – LINKS COURSE

A Tom Morris designed course founded in 1868. It received a James Braid re-design in 1909. Regularly used as a final qualifying course for the Open Championship due to its narrow links fairways, excellent greens and ever-changing wind conditions.

**Website:** www.lundingolfclub.co.uk
**Email:** secretary@lundingolfclub.co.uk
**Telephone:** +44 (0) 1333 320202

**Par:** 71 (White tees) / 73 (Red tees)
**Length:** 5,671yds–6,371yds
**Type:** Links

**Fees:**
▼ per round (weekday & weekend)

Leven Links golf course.

## ● LEVEN LINKS GOLF COURSE

Although the current course layout dates back to 1909, golf at Leven dates back as far as 1820. A series of parallel dune ridges creates an intriguing links challenge with undulating fairways and large true running greens sure to test your nerve with putter in hand.

**Website:** www.leven-links.com
**Email:** secretary@leven-links.com
**Telephone:** +44 (0) 1333 421390

**Par:** 71 (White tees) / 73 (Red tees)
**Length:** 5,775yds–6,551yds
**Type:** Links

**Fees:**
▼ per round (weekday & weekend)

**Visitor Tee Times –**
Monday to Friday after 9.30 am
Saturday after 12.00 noon
Sunday after 10.30 am

## ● CHARLETON GOLF CLUB

Opened in 1994 by former United States President, George H.W. Bush. Set within the Charleton Estate and regarded as one of the most beautiful inland courses in Scotland.

**Website:** www.charleton.co.uk
**Email:** clubhouse@charleton.co.uk
**Telephone:** +44 (0) 1333 340505

**Par:** 72 (White tees) / 71 (Red tees)
**Length:** 5,477yds–6,446yds
**Type:** Parkland

**Fees:**
▼ per round (weekday & weekend)

**9**

## GULLANE GOLF CLUB – COURSE NO. 1

West Links Road,
Gullane,
East Lothian
EH31 2BB
**www.gullanegolfclub.com**
**Phone:** +44 (0) 1620 842 255
**Email:** info@gullanegolfclub.com

**Essential course details –**
**Par:** 71 (Yellow tees) / 74 (Red tees)
**S.S.S:** 71 (Yellow tees) / 75 (Red tees)
**Slope rating:** 129 (White tees)
**Length:** 5,903yds–6,162yds
**Longest hole:** par-5 15th, 466yds–487yds
**Shortest hole:** par-3 4th, 127yds–134yds
**Type:** Links

**Handicap Certificate:** Required (maximum 24 for men and 30 for ladies.)

**Green fees:**
▼: per round (weekday & weekend)

**Caddies:**
£50 – per player per round (+ gratuity) Caddie requests should be made in advance via bookings@ gullanegolfclub.com or telephone 44 (0) 1620 843 767.

**Equipment hire:**
£40 – clubs
£30 – buggies
£15 – motorised trolleys
£5 – push trolleys

To make an equipment booking email admin@gullaneproshop.com or telephone 44 (0) 1620 843 111

### How do I book a round of golf?
Gullane Golf Club is a private members club, however visitors are welcome to play Course No. 1 weekdays – 10.48 am to 12.00 noon and 2.30 pm to 4.00 pm and weekends –10.56 am & 11.04 am and 2.56 pm to 3.28 pm (no weekend bookings are permitted for January and December)

There are two ways to book a round for Course No. 1 at Gullane –

*Email:*
info@gullanegolfclub.com (include all relevant details – preferred dates/ times, group size etc)

*Phone:*
+44 (0) 1620 842 255 (within seven days of play) / +44 (0) 1620 843767 (more than seven days ahead of play)

In all instances a deposit per person is required when the club confirms the booking. The remaining balance is due fourteen days prior to the date of play.

The 1st green at Course No.1 with the 2nd fairway behind, you get a feel for the ascent towards the summit of Gullane Hill. *Gullane Golf Club.*

## HISTORY

In 1882, eight gentlemen of Gullane met to discuss the state of their links and all agreed that to keep them in good order, a club should be formed – The Gullane Golf Club. Originally 32 local golfers became members, growing to 125 a year later. There are now over 1,200 members.

At the time the current courses were being formed, golf at the site was under serious threat from horse racing. Gullane Hill was seen as the perfect exercise area for the horses (hence why the 3rd hole on No.1 is called Racecourse). This practice was finally prohibited in 1892, securing the area for the sole purpose of golf. By 1910 there were three 18-hole courses plus a children's course at the site.

Gullane No. 1 is the oldest course by fourteen years. Established in 1884 it offers a unique links challenge. Gullane No. 2 followed in 1898 and is renowned for a series of testing short holes. In 1910 Gullane No.3 was completed and is also considered a real test for golfers of all abilities.

The 2018 Scottish Open, won by Brandon Stone, utilised a composite course using sixteen holes from Course No. 1 and 2 holes from No. 2.

Stunning aerial view of the par-3 9th hugging the coastline. The green surrounded by bunkers makes for a demanding tee-shot.
*Gullane Golf Club.*

## PLAYING THE COURSE

Gullane No. 1 may not be the most imaginative name for a course but it is, without doubt, an extremely fascinating and unique experience. The course winds its way up, over and around Gullane Hill creating a varied requirement for both downhill and uphill shot making. Gullane is renowned for the quality of its fast-running greens all year round.

If you can avoid the numerous bunkers (the first of 127 on the course) then hole 1 is a gift, 287-yard par-4 with a nice wide fairway. The typically prevailing southwest wind can, however, make the yardage feel a lot longer. For those aiming for the green in two, a drive towards the right-hand side opens up the green for your approach. The 2nd hole is only 345yds but normally played into the teeth of the wind. This is where you begin the march up Gullane Hill. With a bottleneck fairway it's very easy to leave yourself short as you climb towards the green, and there is no margin for error in missing either the slim fairway or narrow green right or left. During the Scottish Open this is played as the 1st hole (the 17th on No.1 is also omitted with the 7th and 8th holes on No.2 completing the composite 18).

Hole 3 is a downhill par-5. Aim left with your drive to set up a 2nd shot to

the right and open up the green. The 4th, the first par-3, is a short one requiring accuracy with bunkers at the front and a steep banking surrounding the entire green. The 5th hole is the toughest on the course – 436-yard par-4 dogleg left, all uphill. Downhill putts on this green can be terrifying! Hole 6 is a relatively gentle short par-4 bringing you to the summit. Look out for the small stone building to the right of the 6th. This is called the Roundel, and is surely the world's smallest golf clubhouse.

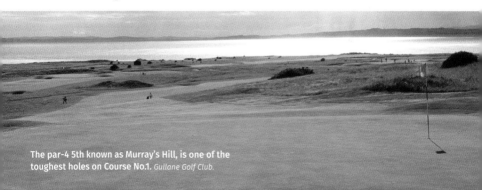

The par-4 5th known as Murray's Hill, is one of the toughest holes on Course No.1. *Gullane Golf Club.*

**(7)** **SIGNATURE HOLE: PAR-4 7TH, 392–398YDS, 'QUEEN'S HEAD'.**
One of the finest views in golf, on a clear day the 360-degree sights
across the Firth of Forth, Edinburgh and Muirfield are heaven sent.

The 7th green lies 398yds away but many feet below you on this
severe downhill hole, giving you a chance to hit a huge drive. However,
there are ten hungry bunkers on this hole, including one each on your
left and right at 181yds, another bunker 241yds away on your left and
yet another 268yds away on your right. Plus there are two at 318yds
just about in the middle to snare those very long hitters who have the
wind at their backs. Hit it straight and you'll be fine.

'Queen's Head' is so called because of the engraving of Queen
Victoria in a rock down the right-hand side of the rough. Local caddies
know where she lives.

The next eight holes are all demanding tests requiring accuracy, focus
and precision. Four, relatively long, par-4s, two par-3s and two tricky par-5s
– including the longest hole on the course (15th), which plays uphill. All are
littered with strategically placed bunkers but generous fairways even things
up with greens accepting of a long iron or fairway wood. On the 12th and 13th

View towards the green at the majestic par-5 12th known as 'The Valley' with
incredible views across to Edinburgh in the distance. *Gullane Golf Club.*

The par-3 13th has bunkers all across the front of the green, so best to aim long here. *Gullane Golf Club.*

enjoy the fine coastal views but also look out for the large concrete stone blocks; these remnants from the Second World War were built to repel Hitler's tanks.

Hole 16 is the final par-3 and, as with the previous short holes, all the trouble lies at the front so make sure you make it onto the green. Use the left-hand bank as a springboard. The 17th offers a similar tee-shot to the 7th taking you steeply down another hill. This is your last chance to hit a big drive and, as the bunkers on this hole all lie beyond 300yds you can really let fly. The 18th is a lovely finishing hole – a short par-4 with a green completely bunker-free. Choose a route that suits your game to avoid the fairway traps and you'll be fine.

Gullane No. 1 may not possess some of the quirks and idiosyncrasies of other links courses but this does not deter from what is a true championship course.

# Other courses on site

In addition to Course No1, Gullane Golf Club also has the following courses available for visitors to play:

## ● COURSE NO. 2 (18 HOLES)

Opened in 1898 and designed by Willie Park Jr, Gullane No. 2 is a charming course with the East Lothian coastline as its backdrop. A shorter but tighter course than No. 1, it is noted for its challenging short holes, epitomised by the 215-yard downhill par-3 11th – one of the most beautiful holes you could ever drop a shot on. Furthermore, the demanding 4th hole is arguably the finest par-4 on all three links. Deer and pheasants abound on the lower section of the course (11th to 14th), especially on an early evening round.

To book a round for Gullane No. 2 follow the same options as detailed for Gullane No. 1. In addition, if you'd prefer to book online this option is also available via the club website for Course No. 2 and Course No. 3.

A day ticket is available to play a combination of courses.

**Par:** 71 (White tees) / 73 (Red tees)
**S.S.S:** 71 (White tees) / 73 (Red tees)
**Length:** 5,566yds–6,385yds

**Green fees:**
▼ per round (weekday & weekend)
▼ day ticket, play No. 1 & No. 2 courses (weekday)
▼ day ticket (weekend)

## ● COURSE NO. 3 (18 HOLES)

Arguably the best views across Aberlady Bay towards Edinburgh and the Firth of Forth can be found at Gullane No. 3. Opened in 1910 and, again, designed by Willie Park Jr. At 5,259yds from the white tees, this is a much shorter course than its older siblings but with sixty-seven bunkers all strategically set and typical fast-running greens this is by no means a soft touch, especially when the wind blows.

Running steeply downhill to a saucer green, the 176-yard par-3 15th is a standout, not just for the stunning views of Gullane and the surrounding East Lothian countryside. Locals will encourage you to hit a chip and run, or even a putter from the tee rather than follow an airborne route to the green.

To book a round for Gullane No. 3 follow the same options as detailed for Gullane No. 2. A day ticket is available to play a combination of courses.

**Par:** 68 (White tees) / 69 (Red tees)
**S.S.S:** 66 (White tees) / 69 (Red tees)
**Length:** 4,920yds–5,259yds

**Green fees:**
▼ per adult (weekday & weekend)
▼ day ticket, play No.1 & No.3 courses (weekday & weekend)
▼ day ticket, play No.2 & No.3 courses (weekday & weekend)

● **CHILDREN'S COURSE**
A six-hole course, opened in 1910, designed specifically for children as

they take their first tentative steps along fairways and begin to hone their putting skills.

Any child can play the course at no cost and booking is not required. Adults must be accompanied by their child.

**Par:** 20
**Length:** 461yds

# 18-hole courses nearby

East Lothian is known as Scotland's Golf Coast due to the wealth of wonderful courses available. Below is a selection of terrific courses within easy driving distance of Gullane.

● **CRAIGIELAW GOLF CLUB**
Designed by Donald Steel and opened in 2001, set in the heart of Scotland's golfing mecca along the East Lothian coastline near to neighbouring Gullane and Muirfield courses.

**Website:** www.craigielawgolfclub.com
**Email:** info@craigielawgolfclub.com
**Telephone:** +44 (0) 1875 870800

**Par:** 71 (White tees) / 71 (Red tees)
**Length:** 5,371yds–6,601yds
**Type:** Links

**Fees:**
▼ per round (weekday & weekend)

● **THE ROYAL MUSSELBURGH GOLF CLUB**
Designed by James Braid, this picturesque parkland course resides at the start of an incredible stretch of golf courses along the East Lothian coastline. It is also home to the oldest trophy still competitively played for in the world – The Old Club Cup (since 1774).

**Website:** www.royalmusselburgh.co.uk
**Email:** managementsecretary@ royalmusselburgh.co.uk
**Telephone:** +44 (0) 1875 819000

**Par:** 70 (White tees) / 73 (Red tees)
**Length:** 5,587yds–6,254yds
**Type:** Parkland

**Fees:**
▼ per round (weekday & weekend)

## THE HONOURABLE COMPANY OF EDINBURGH GOLFERS – MUIRFIELD

Duncur Road,
Muirfield,
Gullane, East Lothian,
Scotland EH31 2EG
**www.muirfield.org.uk**
Phone: +44 (0) 1620 842123
Email: hceg@muirfield.org.uk

**Essential course details –**
**Par:** 71 (White tees) / 76 (Blue tees)
**S.S.S:** 73
**Slope rating:** 142 (White tees) / 132 (Blue tees)
**Length:** 5,980yds–7,245yds
**Longest hole:** Par-5 17th, 460yds–578yds
**Shortest hole:** Par-3 7th, 131yds–187yds
**Type:** Links

**Handicap Certificate:** Required (maximum 18 for men and 20 for ladies)

**Green fees:**
▼ per golfer per round
▼ for two rounds on the same day

**Caddies:**
£50 per round (+gratuity). Strictly one caddie – one golfer policy. Book at least twenty-four hours in advance.

**Equipment hire:**
£40 – buggy (two available on first-come-first-served basis)
FOC – pull trolleys

**How do I book a round of golf?**
**Visitors Playing Days** – Muirfield is a private members Golf Club, however, it welcomes visitors every Tuesday and Thursday throughout the year. Visitors must bring their handicap certificates with them and this must prove they play from a maximum of 18 strokes for men and 20 for ladies.

Play format on the course is fourballs in the morning and foursomes (alternate shot) in the afternoon.

Bookings can be made in advance via the booking system available on the official website – www.muirfield.org.uk.

The system allows you to choose your preferred date from a calendar and, if available, from there you will be placed into direct email contact with the club where you can request confirmation of your booking.

Bookings can be taken up to one year in advance and can also be made via telephone (+44 (0) 1620 842123).

A jacket and tie for gentlemen and smart-casual (non-golfwear) attire for ladies are expected to be worn by all visitors in public rooms within the clubhouse. Lunch is available to all golfers for £30 and is served between 12.30 pm and 3.00 pm.

The view from the tee at the difficult, uphill, par-3 13th at Muirfield. *HCEG Muirfield.*

## HISTORY

The earliest surviving set of golf rules date back to 7 March 1744 and were produced by The Gentlemen Golfers of Leith ahead of a tournament to be held on 2 April of that year. John Rattray, a highly regarded Edinburgh physician, was the first winner of the competition and was awarded with a silver golf club along with the honorary title 'Captain of the Golf'.

There were thirteen rules in total drawn up and overseen by Lord Advocate, Duncan Forbes. While the golf rulebook has grown significantly since, these original rules still form an integral part of the game we now know.

The Gentlemen Golfers of Leith would later become known as The Honourable Company of Edinburgh Golfers from 1800 onwards. Establishing their name would not nearly be as difficult as establishing a permanent base to play. Golf was very popular in the nineteenth century and, having already moved from their Leith origins to Musselburgh, the Honourable Company would again find their home becoming overcrowded, thus, a new site needed to be found.

Further down the coast, the East Lothian racecourse was identified as having all the requirements for a permanent home. The new course would be designed by Old Tom Morris and was named Muirfield. Originally a 16-hole course, opened in May 1891, a swift redesign saw it grow by two further holes in the same year. The Open Championship would be held there in 1892 for the first time and, also for the first time, would be decided over four rounds (72 holes in total).

## PLAYING THE COURSE

Muirfield is unlike any links course, or any course for that matter that you're likely to play. Its layout is unique.

The course is arranged as two loops of nine holes as opposed to the typical links layout where the holes run along the coast and back again creating two sets of nine holes – each set roughly facing in the opposite direction to each other.

Muirfield's outward nine holes follow the perimeter of the course in a clockwise direction whereas the backward nine follow an inner counter-clockwise loop.

### How does this unique layout affect play?

This unparalleled course arrangement creates havoc with wind direction. One hole could be played into a strong wind leading you to believe a one or two club increase is required to get the distance, whereas the next hole may offer a cross-wind challenge, and the next may have the wind behind you. Club selection and ball control becomes absolutely crucial on a hole-by-hole basis.

Muirfield fairways, while deemed fair, leave very little room off the tee as the rough is always left pretty much at one uniform length across the course – long.

While the course is relatively flat compared to other courses in this Guide, don't be fooled into thinking it is a flat course – it is not. There are plenty of areas on the fairways that can leave you with a blind or semi-blind shot into a green.

Every hole represents a unique test, none more so than the short ones – 4th, 7th, 13th and 16th are among the toughest group of par-3s you will find anywhere.

Don't be deceived by the yardage on these holes, from the forward tees they don't appear too frightening, however, they all play to a raised green with lots of bunkers awaiting any stray shot. For example, the 4th has a green shaped like an inverted saucer with three bunkers lurking at the front. A 3-putt here is nailed on if the ball doesn't land firmly from the tee-shot.

The 7th hole plays uphill into the prevailing wind with three bunkers on the left and one front-right. The exposed green, which drops back to front and right to left can also be very quick. The 13th is another uphill tee-shot towards a heavily bunkered green. The 16th is the toughest of the quartet. Don't try and be a hero with your club choice, use whatever it takes to land in the middle of the green.

Also, be prepared to use the dreaded mid-irons off the fairway. Muirfield has a number of long par-4s – and they play long, too. With this in mind, any second shots finishing short of the greens will require a careful short chip to get within 2-putt territory.

Jack Nicklaus has reputedly said the 8th hole at Muirfield is his favourite par-4 in the world. Aim left with your drive on this dogleg right fairway. This is the best set up for a tough approach over the bunkers sitting 50yds out from the front of the green.

**18 SIGNATURE HOLE: PAR-4 18TH, 324–473YDS.**
Possibly the greatest finishing hole in Scotland. With the Clubhouse right in front of you, your tee-shot must tackle the tricky cross-winds coming from the right that will try and push your ball towards two well placed bunkers at the narrowest part of the fairway. The approach shot needs to be clear of two large bunkers sat either side of a long, rising green.

A deep bunker greets you at the 18th green in front of the Clubhouse. *HCEG Muirfield.*

# 18-hole courses nearby

East Lothian is known as Scotland's Golf Coast due to the wealth of wonderful courses available. Below is a selection of terrific courses within easy driving distance of Muirfield.

## ● KILSPINDIE GOLF CLUB

A real hidden gem along the Golf Coast but one definitely worth seeking out during a visit. The course opens with a par-3 on the 1st hole followed by the only par-5 on the course at the 2nd. A tough start to what should be a very enjoyable round of golf.

**Website:** www.kilspindiegolfclub.co.uk
**Email:** bookingenquiry@ kilspindiegolfclub.co.uk
**Telephone:** +44 (0) 1875 870358

**Par:** 69 (Yellow tees) / 70 (Red tees)
**Length:** 5,107yds–5,502yds
**Type:** Links

**Fees:**
▼ per round (weekday & weekend)

## ● LONGNIDDRY GOLF CLUB

A unique blend of parkland and links, located towards the western end of the Golf Coast. There are no par-5s from the yellow tees but there is an abundance of par-4s in excess of 400 yards to contend with.

**Website:** www.longniddrygolfclub.co.uk

**Email:** secretary@longniddrygolfclub. co.uk
**Telephone:** +44 (0) 1875 852141

**Par:** 68 (Yellow tees) / 73 (Red tees)
**Length:** 5,785yds–6,044yds
**Type:** Parkland / Links

**Fees:**
▼ per round (weekday & weekend)

## ● THE MUSSELBURGH GOLF CLUB

Offering a good variety of long and short holes. There's a number of aquatic hazards at play around the course, in particular the Craigie Burn which snakes its way across a number of fairways tempting you into either hitting over or laying up just in front.

**Website:** www. themusselburghgolfclub.com
**Email:** secretary@ themusselburghgolfclub.com
**Telephone:** +44 (0) 131 665 2005

**Par:** 69 (Yellow tees) / 75 (Red tees)
**Length:** 5,680yds–6,241yds
**Type:** Parkland

**Fees:**
▼ per round (weekday & weekend) (the course is not available to visitors on Saturdays)

**11**

# KINGSBARNS GOLF LINKS

Kingsbarns,
St Andrews,
KY16 8QD
**www.kingsbarns.com**
**Phone:** + 44 (0) 1334 460860
**Email:** info@kingsbarns.com

---

**Essential course details –**
**Par:** 72 (All tees)
**S.S.S:** 73 (White tees) / 71 (Red tees)
**Slope:** 138 (White tees) / 126 (Red tees)
**Length:** 5,257yds–6,842yds
**Longest hole:** Par-5 12th, 442yds–566yds
**Shortest hole:** Par-3 8th, 110yds–154yds
**Type:** Links

---

**Handicap Certificate:** Not required.

**Green fees:**
▼ per golfer per round
▼ replay round within seven days
▼ junior golfers (under-18)
▼ PGA / BIGGA members

**Caddies:**
£55 per golfer (+ gratuity).
Forecaddies are available for between
2–4 players at a cost of £80 per round
(+ gratuity). Must book in advance.

**Equipment hire:**
£35 – clubs
£18 – electric trolley
£10 – shoes

## How do I book a round of golf?

The course is unavailable for play
during the winter months, typically
closing between mid-November
until the end of March (check course
website for details).

There are three ways to book a
round of golf at Kingsbarns Golf Links.
It is recommended to book well in
advance.

*Online:*
Make a request via the online
booking form on the official website
– www.kingsbarns.com / booking-
enquiries

*Phone:*
+44 (0) 1334 460861

*Email:*
info@kingsbarns.com

In the case of both email and online,
all booking requests are expected
to receive a response within twenty-
four hours during the season. Also,
during the season, there is a last
minute booking service available
online for tee-times three days in
advance. All payments are expected
to be completed in full at the time of
booking.

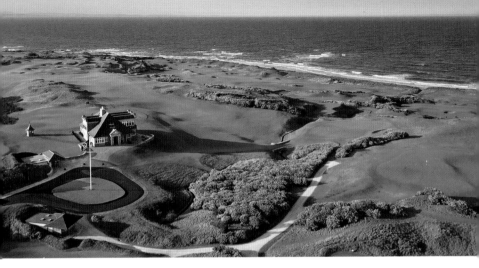

**The Clubhouse at Kingsbarns with the 18th green on the right.**
*Kingsbarns Golf Links.*

## HISTORY

The earliest, recorded, formation of the Kingsbarns Golf Society dates back to 1815 where the Fife and Kinross Almanac states there were forty members and a further forty honorary members. There is evidence suggesting the society actually dates back further.

On 4 September 1793, Crail Golfing Society makes mention in the minutes of a meeting agreeing, 'that members of the Kingsbarns Golfing Society be allowed to appear on the links at crail in the uniform belonging to their own society, Blue Jackets.'(Source: www.scottishgolfinghistory.org)

The original course was only 9 holes, stretched out over the Cambo Estate owned by the Earl of Kellie. To show their gratitude, the members presented the earl with the Erskine Cup in 1826. The club members would meet four times a year to contest various medal tournaments. In 1841, the winner of the Fielden medal is recorded as Mr Robert Haig – grandfather of Field-Marshal Earl Haig who himself would go on to become Captain of the Royal and Ancient Golf Club in 1920.

In 1844 the land would be ploughed over having been deemed too valuable for golf by the owners. By 1922, at the urging of Lady Erskine of Cambo, the society would re-form on the site as Kingsbarns Golf Club, again with a 9-hole course. By 1939 the land would be commandeered again, this time to aid the war effort, and the area was mined as part of the national defence campaign.

Despite numerous attempts, the links laid barren until the end of the twentieth century when American architect Kyle Phillips took on the challenge of designing a new course. Opened in July 2000 with a layout remaining true to the links traditions laid down hundreds of years before, many who visit fail to notice just how recently the course was completed.

## PLAYING THE COURSE

With views of the North Sea from virtually every part of the course, the Cambo burn (uncovered during the build), rippling fairways with plenty of humps and hollows and howling wind from different directions during the round. Six miles along the coast from St Andrews, Kingsbarns is a phenomenal links test.

The round starts with a 400-yard par-4 slight dogleg right. If you're a long hitter, aim left from the tee to avoid the two hidden fairway bunkers at around 280yds. A strong cross-wind can wreak havoc with your approach shot. The green slopes back to front so a long hit towards the back should roll towards the pin.

With 200yds to the back of the green and stunning views of Carnoustie across the Firth of Tay, the 2nd hole requires focus and favours a shot towards

**Stunning aerial view of the 7th, 8th, 11th and 15th holes at Kingsbarns.** *Kingsbarns Golf Links.*

the left-hand side although be aware of the hidden greenside bunker if the pin is cut towards that side when you play.

Hole 3 is a short par-5. Located at the foot of a hill on the left with the sea to the right, aim left from the tee to stay out of trouble. Another green that requires plenty of club to avoid the bunkers on the right, or lay up short for a chip on to the putting surface.

The next four holes are all par-4s of varying lengths. Hole 6 is driveable with a real risk and reward flavour to it; 280yds from tee to the back of the green, but with a water hazard directly behind (the sea!). The green has two levels and slopes front to back. This hole can turn from birdie opportunity to a nightmare very easily as everything moves towards a miss hit into the water. You've been warned!

## 12) SIGNATURE HOLE: PAR-5 12TH, 442–566YDS 'ORRDEAL'.

The back-nine eases you toward home with two more par-4s before the stunning par-5 12th. At 566yds it is the longest hole on the course. Aim to the right from the tee and second shot, as the slope should bring the ball back towards the centre of the fairway. The green is long, but with numerous bunkers front and back care is needed with any short chipping.

Hole 7 is the toughest on the course and its name – Lang Wynd – translates as 'narrow street'. Aim right from the tee and take an extra club for each approach shot as the hole moves uphill toward the green.

The longest hole is followed by the shortest but don't let the distance fool you on hole 13. Anything missed to the right leaves a difficult second shot.

The par-4 15th offers another stunning scene with the sea bashing against the shoreline to your right. Most right-handers will need huge focus here. Aim for the left fairway bunker at around 200yds and let the ball drift in to the centre from there, leaving you with a clear shot into the green. The woods to the left will block out the wind so try not to over compensate too much.

The round concludes with another tricky par-4. Aim for the left-hand corner of the clubhouse to avoid the fairway bunkers on the left. The approach shot to the green needs to be a confident one as you clear the burn at the front. You could lay up in front of the burn but the ground can quickly draw the ball into the water. It's your last approach shot on this wonderful course – be brave! 12.

The 15th fairway curves along the coast up to the green. *Kingsbarns Golf Links.*

Golfers about to make their approach shot to the 17th green. *Kingsbarns Golf Links.*

**12**

## THE MACHRIHANISH GOLF CLUB – CHAMPIONSHIP COURSE

Golf Club House,
Machrihanish,
Argyll,
Scotland, PA28 6PT
**www.machgolf.com**
**Phone:** +44 (0) 1586 810213 Option 1
**Email:** secretary@machgolf.com

**Essential course details –**
**Par:** 70 (White tees) / 72 (Red tees)
**S.S.S:** 71 (White tees) / 72 (Red tees)
**Slope rating:** 131 (White tees) / 129 (Red tees)
**Length:** 5,497yds–6,462yds
**Longest hole:** Par-5 12th, 'Long Hole', 456yds–510yds
**Shortest hole:** Par-3 4th, 'Jura', 110yds–131yds
**Type:** Links

**Handicap Certificate:** Required (maximum 28 for men and 36 for ladies)

**Green fees:**
▼ per round (low/shoulder/high season)

**Caddies:**
£45 per person (+ gratuity). Must be booked when booking your round

**Equipment hire:**
£30 buggies
Club and pull trolley hire also available via Pro shop.

### How do I book a round of golf?
There are three ways to book a round of golf for the Championship Course at Machrihanish:

*Online:*
www.machgolf.com – tee reservations

*Phone:*
+44 (0) 1586 810277

*Email:*
pro@machgolf.com (include all relevant details – preferred dates/times, group size etc)

### HISTORY
Before the formation of any club, golf had been played at Machrihanish since 1871. It would be another five years before a meeting was held at the Argyll Arms Hotel on 11 March 1876, the sole purpose of which was to establish an official Golf Club in Campbeltown. The club was originally known as The Kintyre Golf Club.

The Machrihanish course originally consisted of 10 holes, then extended to 12 holes under the guidance of Charles Hunter from Prestwick.

**The 10th green sits amongst cavernous, rolling, terrain.** *Machrihanish Golf Club.*

Finally, in 1879, the club sought advice from none other than Old Tom Morris when completing its expansion from 12 to the full 18 holes.

After this last extension, Old Tom played a round at the course, competing against other luminaries of the time – Jim Morris, Bob Martin from St Andrews and Jack Morris of Hoylake – with a prize of £10 for the winner (not an insignificant amount in those days). Jim Morris would emerge triumphant with a score of 78.

Following his round, Old Tom Morris would utter an immortal line about Machrihanish, which still resonates today: 'specifically designed by The Almighty for playing golf'. (Source: www.machgolf.com)

By the end of the nineteenth century the club had well over 300 members, many of which were based in Glasgow, Edinburgh and even London. During 1914 the course would undergo further re-designs by both J.H. Taylor and, soon afterwards, Sir Guy Campbell. These alterations were the last major renovations to the course as it stands today.

## PLAYING THE COURSE

We all wish we had all the time in the world when we play a round of golf. It's not just the actual play we wish we had time for but also time to hit some practice balls beforehand and, perhaps, warm our putter up before we step onto the course. The reality is most of us pull up in our car, put on our shoes, grab our bag and are still ferreting around for our ball, tees, pitch repairer and marker while we walk to the first tee.

Most courses will settle you in gently so you can afford to make your first shot completely 'cold'. No such luck at Machrihanish, so make sure you're ready. The first hole at the Championship Course is considered one of the very best and most daunting first holes anywhere in the world. When you get to the first tee, you'll see why.

**How's your nerve? The view from the world famous 1st tee at Machrihanish.**
*Machrihanish Golf Club.*

**① SIGNATURE HOLE: PAR-4 1ST, 422–436YDS, 'THE BATTERY'.**
If there's a scarier first tee-shot than the one here, it would be hard to imagine how so. Standing between the tee box and the fairway lays the Atlantic Ocean. You must decide how much of the shoreline you're prepared to take on to get your ball closer to the green for the approach shot. Typically, you'll need to look at distances of at least 150yds.

The good news is, if you land on the sand your ball is playable from there – it is not out of bounds. If you do miss the fairway, take solace in the fact you were not the first and you most definitely will not be the last.

Hole 3 is regarded as true championship quality. The 373-yard par-4 has some strategically placed bunkers protecting the green from around 50yds out. The front-9 holes are all par-4s of varying lengths with the exception of the shortest hole on the course, the par-3 4th. Despite being no longer than 121yds from the back tees, you need to hit an accurate low-iron shot to make it over two bunkers protecting the front of an elevated green and one on your right-hand side.

The 5th hole is another classic links layout with plenty of rough between the tee box and the fairway. Once on the fairway there are plenty of humps and hollows to navigate before reaching the green.

The back-9 holes offer a greater selection with two par-5s, three par-3s and four par-4s. The 10th is another great links hole – a clever dogleg par-5 with two bunkers protecting the front of the green. Hole 14 plays as the most difficult on the course; it looks pretty straight and only has one bunker on the left of the green, but at 459 yards it can be a real stretch to make the green in two shots.

The 16th is a 232-yard par-3 normally playing into the prevailing wind and is often a driver to even get close to the green. Finally, holes 17 and 18 favour the brave, with out of bounds down the left (never easy with a card in your hand).

It's a long journey to play the championship course at Machrihanish but the first tee-shot will live with you all the way back home.

**The sun begins to set over the 18th green.**
*Machrihanish Golf Club.*

# Other courses on site

In addition to the championship course, The Machrihanish Golf Club also has the following course available for visitors to play:

### ● PANS COURSE (9 HOLES)

Named after the Old Salt Pans at Machrihanish. No need to book in advance, and after a long journey, it's well worth taking the time to play 9 holes at the Pans Course while you're in town.

**Par:** 34

**Length:** 2,319yds–2,376yds

**Green fees:**

▼ per round (weekday & weekend) (9-hole price guide)

# 18-hole courses nearby

### ● MACHRIHANISH DUNES

Described as the most natural course in the world and the only course ever constructed on a site of special scientific interest (SSSI). Opened in 2009, only 7 acres, from a total of 259, were disturbed during construction. Only the greens and tees were shaped, the fairways were simply mowed to the appropriate length.

**Website:** www.machrihanishdunes.com
**Email:** info@machdunes.com
**Phone:** +44 (0) 1586 810001 (International) / 0800 151 3701 (UK)

**Par:** 72
**Length:** 5,076yds–7,082yds
**Type:** Links

**Fees:**

▼ per round (weekday & weekend)
▼ day pass

### ● DUNAVERTY GOLF CLUB

A natural links course with spectacular views over the surrounding landscape. A rare overall par of 66 includes seven par-3s and just one par-5.

**Website:** www.dunavertygolfclub.com
**Email:** dunavertygc@aol.com
**Phone:** +44 (0) 1586 830677

**Par:** 66
**Length:** 4,577yds–4,799yds
**Type:** Links

**Fees:**

▼ per round (weekday & weekend)

**13**

# THE NAIRN GOLF CLUB – THE CHAMPIONSHIP COURSE

The Nairn Golf Club,
Seabank Road,
Nairn,
IV12 4HB
**www.nairngolfclub.co.uk**
**Phone:** +44 (0) 1667 453208
**Email:** bookings@nairngolfclub.co.uk

## Essential course details –

**Par:** 72 (Blue tees) / 75 (Red tees)
**S.S.S:** 74 (Blue tees) / 75 (Red tees)
**Slope rating:** 137 (Blue tees) / 139 (Red tees)
**Length:** 5,735yds–6,774yds
**Longest hole:** Par-5 18th, 463yds–554yds
**Shortest hole:** Par-3 4th, 132yds–160yds
**Type:** Links

**Handicap Certificate:** Required (maximum 28 for men and 36 for ladies)

### Green fees –
▼ per round (High season)
▼ per round (Shoulder season)
▼ per round (Low season)
▼ per round (Junior 17 & under)
▼ two rounds (played over 4-day period)

**Caddies:**
£45 per player per round (+gratuity). Forecaddie available for £70 per group per round (+gratuity)

**Equipment hire –**
£15 electric trolley
£35 club hire (plus 3 golf balls)
£35 electric buggy (medical certificate required)

### How do I book a round of golf?
Nairn Golf Club is a private members club, however, visitor bookings are available for the Championship Course on the following times during the week –
Monday–Thursday after 9.30 am
Friday after 10.00 am
Weekends after 11.00 am
There are three ways to book a round of golf for The Championship Course at Nairn Golf Club.

*Online:*
www.nairngolfclub.co.uk – click on the 'BOOK TEE TIMES' button at the top right of the main home page

*Phone:*
+44 (0) 1667 453208

*Email:*
bookings@nairngolfclub.co.uk (include all relevant details – preferred dates/times, group size etc)

## HISTORY

The Nairn Golf Club was established in 1887. The local MP, Robert Finlay, was the mastermind behind the creation of the club. Finlay was born in Edinburgh and despite becoming a medical graduate he would pursue a very successful legal career. Appointed as a QC in 1882, Solicitor General in 1892 and by 1900, Attorney General for England and Wales. His career culminated with his rise to the position of Lord Chancellor from 1916 to 1919 in Lloyd George's coalition government. Upon retirement he was created Viscount Finlay of Nairn in the County of Nairn.

Finlay used his considerable influence to persuade many London-based friends to come north and join as members of the Golf Club. Archie Simpson – Keeper of the Green at Royal Aberdeen – designed the original course before Finlay called upon the expertise of Old Tom Morris, the doyen of course designers.

A further twenty years would pass before more revisions were required, this time from another esteemed designer – James Braid. Despite some modest tinkering and lengthening prior to the 1999 Walker Cup, the course remains true to Braid's final design.

The 1999 Walker Cup would bring the GB & I team only their fifth victory in the competition spanning nearly eighty years. The first and, to date, only time the event was held at Nairn also featured two young up and coming golfers – Luke Donald and Paul Casey – who secured a comprehensive 15–9 victory for the home nations.

## PLAYING THE COURSE

Every hole on The Championship Course offers you a view of the Moray Firth as you play. True to its Scottish links heritage, the fairways require accuracy from tee to green with lots of heavy gorse on one side and water on the other. However, many who have played here – including James Braid – will tell you it's the greens themselves that are the real test of this course.

Seven of the first nine holes are played into the wind with the first being Hole 1. The sea is a lateral hazard from the 1st to the 7th hole, however, on the 1st it would take a wild drive to the right for it to come into play. Two left-hand fairway bunkers need to be avoided from the tee before an approach shot into a fairly flat and open green.

Hole 2 has a ditch running across the fairway at just over 300yds, so any long hitters should beware. There are also bunkers left and right before that so an accurate drive is required. Hole 3, another par-4, is another tight fairway

**Looking straight down the fairway from the 2nd green.**
*Mark Alexander Golf Photography.*

with a slight dogleg left. All the trouble sits toward the front of the green so you can be brave with your approach shot.

Hole 4 is the first par-3 and the shortest hole on the course. A long narrow green with bunkers front right and the sea to the left. The next par-3, hole 6, is one of the most challenging as the tee-shot needs to carry all the way to the green with bunkers surrounding the front.

Hole 7 is a tough par-5 with two fairway bunkers waiting left and right for any stray tee-shots at around 260yds. The second shot needs to navigate a further bunker sat right in the middle of the fairway before the green. Two more par-4s await before the turn – both look driveable but are much trickier than they seem.

Once you've stopped for refreshments at the historic Bothy, originally used for storing salmon, it's on to the testing par-5 10th. Thick bushes all along the right of the fairway and heavy rough along the left mean only a straight drive will do. Keep it straight all the way to the green and you're fine.

Hole 12 starts a stretch of three challenging holes. The 13th is definitely unlucky for some and considered the hardest hole on the course. A bunker sits just left of the fairway in the exact position where you will want to hit your drive. The green is very undulating leaving a very fast putt for a well-earned par.

**14 SIGNATURE HOLE: PAR-3 14TH, 177–219YDS 'KOPJES'.**
Hole 14 offers an elevated tee-shot with spectacular views, however, don't be shy on taking your driver out here as a long carry, with a strong cross-wind, is needed to reach the green. This is the hole that will make you want to come back and play here again and again.

After three testing par-4s – you finish the round with a long par-5 at the 18th. Playing downwind this is one of the few holes with a genuine safe-side all along the left. This hole offers a great opportunity to finish with a good score and one to remember, but as always – hit it straight.

The best-guarded green on the course at the 16th. *Mark Alexander Golf photography.*

A deep bunker awaits any stray tee shots at the short par-4 17th. *Mark Alexander Golf photography.*

# Other courses on site

In addition to The Championship Course, Nairn Golf Club also has the following course available for visitors to play:

● **THE CAMERON COURSE (9 HOLES)**
The nine-hole Cameron Course provides a good practice ground for any golfer about to head out on to the championship course. Alternatively, the course is a fun way for youngsters to find their range with a set of clubs. With two par-4s included, the Cameron provides a solid test and a lot of fun.

**Par:** 29
**Length:** 1,634yds

**Green fees:**
▼ day ticket
(9-hole price guide)

# 18-hole courses nearby

● **NAIRN DUNBAR GOLF CLUB – LINKS COURSE**
Situated behind the rugged sand dunes of the town's East Beach, Nairn Dunbar is a championship-length layout featuring a terrific range of par-4s, some tough short holes and four demanding par-5s including both at the 9th and 18th. With views across the Moray Firth to the Black Isle, it's a course not to be missed.

**Website:** www.nairndunbar.com
**Email:** secretary@nairndunbar.com
**Telephone:** +44 (0) 1667 452741

**Par:** 72 (White tees) / 75 (Red tees)
**Length:** 5,748yds–6,290yds
**Type:** Links

**Fees:**
▼ per round (weekday & weekend)
▼ Nairn ticket (one round at Nairn & one round at Nairn Dunbar).

## NORTH BERWICK GOLF CLUB – THE WEST LINKS COURSE

The North Berwick Golf Club
New Club House,
Beach Road,
North Berwick,
East Lothian,
EH39 4BB
www.northberwickgolfclub.com
Phone: +44 (0) 1620 895040
Email: bookings@
northberwickgolfclub.com

**Essential course details –**

**Par:** 71 (Blue tees) / 74 (Red tees)

**S.S.S:** 72 (Blue tees) / 74 (Red tees)

**Slope rating:** 127 (Blue tees) / 131 (Red tees)

**Length:** 5,755yds–6,140yds

**Longest hole:** Par-5 11th, 459yds–526yds

**Shortest hole:** par-3 6th, 124yds–139yds

**Type:** Links

**Handicap Certificate:** Required (maximum 24 for men and 36 for ladies)

### Green fees:
▼ per round (Mon–Fri & Sunday)
▼ Full day
(1 April–31 October)
▼ per round (Mon–Fri & Sunday)
(1 November – 17 December)
50 per cent – junior green fees apply

(17 and under with valid handicap certificate)

### Caddies:
£50 per caddie per player (+ gratuity). Book in advance.

### Equipment hire:
£35 – clubs per player per round, available for left and right-handers.

The club does not have any carts/buggies for hire, however, visitors are able to bring their own single seat cart/buggy for use on the course if required.

### How do I book a round of golf?
The North Berwick Golf Club is a private members club however visitors are welcome to play the course Monday, Wednesday and Friday from 10.36 am until 2.57 pm and on Tuesdays and Thursdays from 10.36 am to 4.09 pm (unless playing 36 holes when times are available from 10.09 am) and from 12:36 pm on Sundays. Play on a Saturday is as a guest of a member only.

There are three ways to book a round of golf for The West Links Course at North Berwick:

*Online:*
www.northberwickgolfclub.com

*Phone:*
+44 (0) 1620 892135

*Email:*
bookings@northberwickgolfclub.
com (include all relevant details –
preferred dates/times, group size etc)
    In all instances a deposit of
£30 per person is required when
the club confirms the booking.
The remainder can be paid to the
starter on the day or online prior to
your visit. If paying the starter, leave
plenty of time before the start of
the round.

## HISTORY

There are four private members clubs who play their golf on the West Links
course. Tantallon Golf Club (founded 1853), Bass Rock Golf Club (founded 1873),
The North Berwick Ladies' Golf Club (founded 1888) and The North Berwick
Golf Club – the oldest of the quartet having begun life at exactly noon on 4
June 1832.

    Originally opened as a 6-hole course, it would be a further forty-five years
before the course was extended to a full
18 holes in 1877. However, with 7 holes
totalling 200yds or less, further expansion
was required and was completed in 1895
resulting in a far tougher challenge as
the total yardage reached 6,095yds. The
present layout and shape of the course
owes its dues to the last significant
alterations made in 1932.

    North Berwick also has the distinction
of only ever having employed two golf
professionals during its history. In 1967 the
club appointed David Huish who remained
Head Professional until 2009. Upon
retirement David handed over the reigns
to his son, Martyn. The Pro shop was the
original factory where Ben Sayer, biggest
club exporter to the US at the time, plied
his trade.

    Possibly the most famous member, and
one who would attract many other famous
people of the time, was a local landowner
who became captain of The North Berwick

**The green at the tricky par-4 7th.**
*Mark Alexander Golf Photography.*

Golf Club in 1899 – Arthur James Balfour. Between 1902–06, Balfour was prime minister of Great Britain.

In 1903, on one particular day there were, in course of play at the same time on the West Links, the prime minister, the Speaker of the House of Commons, four members of parliament, two bishops of the Church of England, three eminent professors, a field marshal, two generals and a famous Tibetan explorer.

## PLAYING THE COURSE

If you believe golf should be played for the sheer enjoyment of it all, then get ready to have some fun.

It is said that in order to play The West Links course a golfer must have in their possession a sense of humour. Occasionally overshadowed by some of its coastal neighbours as a contender for the crown of 'toughest test in links golf', nevertheless The West Links Course holds a special place in the hearts of those who have played it.

From rock walls traversing alongside and across holes, huge swales that dissect greens, the Firth of Forth offering incredible views out to Craigleith Island and Bass Rock, this is a course that offers immense pleasure from beginning to end.

The West Links course is as true a links course as you will find and shares some similar traits with the Old Course, St Andrews. The course starts in town and finishes back in town. The last hole is a driveable par-4 with the green right in front of the clubhouse. It's also right next to the shoreline – you simply couldn't get any closer to it.

Usually the front-nine plays into a prevailing wind and the back-nine with the wind behind.

The first thing to note is the distance – it is, by no means, the longest links course in the world and with the fairway-rough kept purposely short in order to speed up play, stray shots should not suffer any undue punishment. The 1st hole, a par-4 just over 300yds, offers an immediate chance to drive onto the green – the largest on the course. For those not blessed with such capabilities, aim for the path that cuts across the fairway at circa 200yds before aiming your approach shot left of the pin.

Hole 2 dares you to drive across the sea. It's longer than it looks so be careful how much of the beach you cut off. Hole 3 is the toughest hole on the course – and what a test. You need to aim your drive towards a gap in the wall that sits in front of you and the approach shot must go over the wall but steer clear of the bunker on the right of the green.

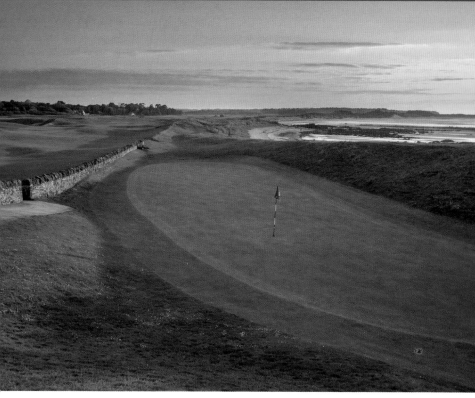

**The 13th green protected by a wall requiring a good chip over with a short iron.** *Mark Alexander Golf Photography.*

Holes 4 and 6 are tough par-3s where under-clubbing would be a sin. Hole 8 is the first par-5 test. Be sure to avoid the fairway bunkers on the left hand side. Hole 9 also offers more trouble on the left of the fairway than the right.

As you move onto the back-9 the wind will become more downwind and this will assist on the par-5 11th and make it feel shorter than it is.

The 13th is where the fun really starts. A short par-4 with a twist ... or, rather, a wall. A straight drive will leave you with a short iron up and over it to the sunken green behind. From this part of the course you also have a perfect view out to Fidra Island, said to be the inspiration for Robert Louis Stevenson's famous novel, *Treasure Island*.

The 14th hole is called 'Perfection' because it requires two perfect shots in order to yield a reward. If you can't manage one after another, make sure the tee-shot is straight.

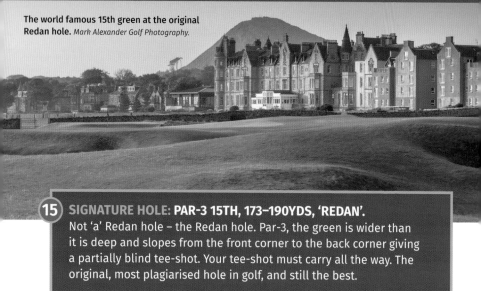

**The world famous 15th green at the original Redan hole.** *Mark Alexander Golf Photography.*

**(15) SIGNATURE HOLE: PAR-3 15TH, 173–190YDS, 'REDAN'.**
Not 'a' Redan hole – the Redan hole. Par-3, the green is wider than it is deep and slopes from the front corner to the back corner giving a partially blind tee-shot. Your tee-shot must carry all the way. The original, most plagiarised hole in golf, and still the best.

Almost as famous as the 15th, hole 16 has the unique 'Biarritz' green – narrow, raised and dissected by a gully. Hole 18 offers a terrific chance of finishing with a flurry right in front of the clubhouse. Give yourself plenty of room on the left to avoid any right-hand slices heading into the car park. No one wants to end their round with a bill for a new windscreen.

# Other courses on site

In addition to the West Links course, North Berwick Golf Club also has the following course available for visitors to play:

### ● THE CHILDREN'S COURSE (9 HOLES)

Established in 1888 as the Ladies Links course, the Children's Course is a 9-hole, par-3 layout located near the 15th and 16th holes of the West Links. An ideal circuit for any youngster wanting to take their first tentative swings around a golf course and hone their craft. Adults must be accompanied by a child when playing the course.

**Par:** 27

For booking enquiries contact the club either via email (bookings@ northberwickgolfclub.com) or phone (+44 (0) 1620 892135).

# 18-hole courses nearby

East Lothian is known as Scotland's Golf Coast due to the wealth of wonderful courses available. Below is a selection of terrific courses within easy driving distance of North Berwick.

### ● GLEN GOLF CLUB – EAST LINKS

Just around the corner from North Berwick, the Glen offers breathtaking views from its clifftop location out to Bass Rock and the Firth of Forth. Originally opened as a nine-hole course in 1894, it was extended to 18 holes in 1906 following a redesign by James Braid and Ben Sayers.

**Website:** www.glengolfclub.co.uk
**Email:** enquiries@glengolfclub.co.uk
**Telephone:** +44 (0) 1620 892726

**Par:** 70 (Blue tees) / 73 (Red tees)
**Length:** 5,773yds–6,048yds
**Type:** Links

**Fees:**
▼ per round (weekdays & weekend)

### ● DUNBAR GOLF CLUB – EAST LINKS

The last outpost in the East along Scotland's Golf Coast, the Club was founded in 1856 and originally played its golf on a rudimentary 15-hole course. In 1894 Old Tom Morris was called upon to weave his magic and in 1923 Ben Sayers and James Braid offered some more advice on bunker placement resulting in the installation of a further sixty-one sand traps.

The course lies along a narrow strip of land between an old deer sanctuary and the rugged coastline which sits tightly alongside. A classic links course and one well worth making the trip across for.

**Website:** www.dunbargolfclub.com
**Email:** secretary@dunbargolfclub.com
**Telephone:** +44 (0) 1368 862317

**Par:** 71 (White tees) / 72 (Red tees)
**Length:** 5,783yds–6,404yds
**Type:** Links

**Fees:**
▼ per round (Mon-Wed/Friday)
▼ per round (weekend)
(no visitor tee-times are available on Thursdays)

## PRESTWICK GOLF CLUB – THE LINKS

2–4 Links Road,
Prestwick,
Ayrshire,
KA9 1QG
**www.prestwickgc.co.uk**
Phone: +44 01292 477404
Email: secretary@prestwickgc.co.uk

**Essential course details –**

**Par:** 71 (White tees) / 74 (Green tees)

**S.S.S:** 73 (White tees) / 74 (Green tees)

**Slope rating:** 133 (White tees) / 132 (Green tees)

**Length:** 5,571yds–6,551yds

**Longest hole:** Par-5 12th, 452yds–513yds

**Shortest hole:** Par-3 2nd, 123yds–164yds

**Type:** Links

**Handicap Certificate:** Required (maximum of 24 for men and 28 for ladies)

### Green fees:

▼ per round (weekdays)
▼ per round (weekend)

### Caddies:

Highly recommended for first time visitors to the course.
£50 per caddie per round (+ gratuity). Forecaddie's available, £70 per group per round (+gratuity)

### Equipment hire:

£50 – clubs per round
£20 – electric trolley
£6 – pull trolley
£30.00* – buggy

*= buggies are available, specifically, for anyone with a medical condition. You must take a caddie with you to drive the buggy around the course.

### How do I book a round of golf?

Prestwick Golf Club is a private members club; however, it welcomes visitors at all times during the week except Saturdays. During the summer there may be limited availability on Sundays.

There are three ways to book a round of golf for The Links course at Prestwick:

*Online:*
www.prestwickgc.co.uk/bookings. A deposit of £110 per player is required to confirm the reservation.

*Phone:*
+44 (0) 1292 477404

*Email:*
bookings@prestwickgc.co.uk (include all relevant details – preferred dates/times, group size etc)

**The Prestwick Experience:** a specially priced ticket (£225 – 2019 price) that includes a round of golf and a three-course lunch (excluding drinks) in

**15th green with the Clubhouse in the background.** *Mark Alexander Golf photography.*

the dining room. Numbers are strictly limited to thirty-two each day with four-ball times between 8.00 am and 9.00 am on Wednesdays and Fridays, reserved exclusively for golfers wishing to participate in The Prestwick Experience. Available via email and/or telephone reservation only.

## HISTORY

As the industrial revolution traversed its way through Scotland in the nineteenth century it used the railway as its primary mode of transport. A few years after the tracks had been laid between Glasgow and Ayr, fifty-seven local golfers met on 2 July 1851 at the Red Lion Inn, Prestwick and formed their own Golf Club.

Two cottages were purchased opposite the Inn. One would become the clubhouse and the other was given to the green keeper, Tom Morris who, at the age of 30, had not yet become 'Old' Tom Morris (Young Tom having just been born a few months prior). Both buildings are still in existence today albeit used for different purposes. The original course consisted of only 12-holes, expansion to 18 holes would not be completed until 1882 after further land to the north of the course was purchased.

Prestwick will always be known as the birthplace of The Open Championship. Following the death of Allan Robertson, supreme golfer of his generation, the concept of an 'Open' tournament was raised as a means to find the new champion golfer. From the very first championship played in October 1860 and for the next twelve years, with the exception of 1871 when no championship was played, The Open would be held at Prestwick Golf Club.

Originally the winner was presented with a red Moroccan belt, known as the 'Challenge Belt', until Young Tom Morris won a hat-trick of tournaments (1868–70) and was allowed to keep it. By 1872 agreement had finally been reached between Prestwick, Royal & Ancient and The Honourable Company of Edinburgh Golfers to share hosting for the championship. A brand new trophy was designed and purchased for £30, each club contributing £10. However, this new trophy would not be ready for the 1872 championship, won again by Young Tom, so on this occasion he was presented with a gold medal inscribed 'Golf Champion Trophy' instead.

It was not until 1873 when St Andrews hosted it's first ever Open Championship that the Golf Champion Trophy was awarded to the winner, Tom Kidd. The first name on the trophy, however, is that of Tom Morris, Champion Golfer 1872. This is why at The Open each year the winner is announced as the winner of the gold medal and Champion Golfer of the Year rather than as the Open Champion.

Of course, modern day golf enthusiasts know the Golf Champion Trophy by it's other, more commonly used, name – the Claret Jug.

Ultimately the popularity of the tournament would be the course's undoing. Unable to handle such large crowds, Prestwick would hold its 24th and last Open Championship in 1925. Incredibly, almost 100 years on, only the Old Course, St Andrews, has hosted more.

## PLAYING THE COURSE

The Links course at Prestwick is everything you expect it to be. The entire place has the feel of a traditional monument to golf of yore. If you're looking for the most authentic example of links golf then you need look no further – it's here.

Holes twist and turn through rugged dunes and rippled fairways. Blind

**View from the 1st green back down the fairway towards the Clubhouse with the railway line running along the right-hand side.** *Mark Alexander Golf Photography.*

This is the view that greets golfers at the 5th tee. Your ball needs to clear the hill in front of you to make the green. *Prestwick Golf Club.*

shots over huge, grass-covered, sand dunes. Cavernous bunkers with wooden rickety steps to take you to the bottom. Greens that are firm and fast – some hidden in hollows, others raised up on a plateaux. All are relatively small compared to some of its links counterparts.

The 1st hole is regarded as one of the toughest opening holes in Scotland (or anywhere for that matter). It's only 345yds in length and dead straight – sounds easy, right? Well ... it's called 'Railway' and it has a railway line running along the right-hand side. This creates a nerve-jangling first tee-shot. Do you go with an iron or a 3-wood? Whichever you choose – hit it straight down the middle.

The 3rd is a relatively short par-5 at 477yds, however it is rated as one of the toughest on the course. A sharp dogleg right, the hole is dominated by a cluster of huge bunkers known as the Cardinal bunkers (after the name given to the hole) 230yds from the tee. The temptation to try and hit over the first bunker must be avoided as the next, much larger, bunker lies only 30yds further on and will swallow up your ball, so don't be a hero. The best line is to aim towards the right of the fairway in order to reduce the angle into the green. The Pow burn runs alongside the hole on the right and is out of bounds the entire length.

After the par-4 4th it's on to the world famous par-3 5th. Is there a more daunting blind shot in golf than this? Its name – Himalayas – gives you a taste for what's in store. Club selection is crucial – you must give yourself enough to clear the hill and aim at the coloured sleeper that matches the tee you're playing from. The hole has five bunkers along the left of the green – the prevailing wind will try and push your ball that way. The tee box will show you where the hole is cut. Once you've finished the hole there is a bell that you can ring to inform anyone playing behind that it's clear for them.

Elysian Fields are a stretch of four very testing par-4s from the 6th through to the 9th. Lots of hidden fairway bunkers await any miss-hit shots.

The 12th hole is the longest on the course. Caddies like to joke with first-time visitors if the wind is swirling into your face you'll need a driver, three-wood and a taxi to get up to the green. The last 6 holes are all testing par-4s starting with the 13th. Regardless of the weather a par here should be cherished. A fairway bunker called Willie Campbell's grave sits hidden at 265yds from the tee. Lots of undulating ground will leave you with an uneven stance as you make your way to the green. The 15th hole has the most

## 17 SIGNATURE HOLE: PAR-4 17TH, 372–394YDS, 'ALPS'.

Originally the 2nd hole for the initial 1851 layout, this is, therefore, the oldest existing hole in championship golf.

The 17th is where you'll find the famous Sahara Bunker. Before you get that far, hopefully avoiding it if you can, there's a narrow fairway to navigate requiring accuracy from the tee. Your approach shot is played blind, adding spice to this terrific hole. Check the tee box for the pin positions on that day which will correspond with the markers on top of the Alps. If in doubt take an extra club to be sure.

**17th green with the legendary Sahara Bunker right in front.** *Mark Alexander Golf Photography.*

demanding tee-shot on the entire course. Bunkers sit both right and left ready to swallow up any stray shots from 200yds onwards.

The 18th is regarded as one of the gentlest on the course. Aim for the clock on the clubhouse with your tee-shot and all will be well. An excellent chance to finish a round of golf with a good score.

There are many tougher courses, but no modern-day course can ever replicate what Prestwick has. If you know and respect your golf history, then any course wishlist will never be complete without a round at the birthplace of The Open.

# 18-hole courses nearby

## ● PRESTWICK ST NICHOLAS GOLF CLUB

A brief walk along down the Main Street from its famous older brother you will find St Nicholas Golf Club. Originally known as the Prestwick Mechanics to reflect the profession of its founding fathers, one of whom was the great Tom Morris himself. With many natural hazards and 'out of bounds' featuring on at least 12 holes, this is definitely a course for the more thoughtful golfer rather than those who prefer to swing first, think later.

**Website:** www.prestwickstnicholas.com
**Email:** secretary@ prestwickstnicholas.com
**Telephone:** +44 (0) 1292 477608

**Par:** 69 (White tees) / 72 (Red tees)
**Length:** 5,415yds–6,044yds
**Type:** Links

**Fees:**
▼ per round (weekdays & weekend)

## ● PRESTWICK ST CUTHBERT GOLF CLUB

St Cuthbert Golf Club originally played its golf further north, however, the current course was opened in 1963 to make way for the development of Glasgow Airport. Now fully matured this is a beautiful parkland course with fabulous greens and trees lining picturesque fairways. A real challenge and a great addition alongside its links cousins just down the road.

**Website:** www.stcuthbert.co.uk
**Email:** secretary@stcuthbert.co.uk
**Telephone:** +44 (0) 1292 477101

**Par:** 70 (Yellow tees) / 71 (Red tees)
**Length:** 5,292yds–5,993yds
**Type:** Parkland

**Fees:**
▼ per round (weekdays & weekend)

## ROYAL ABERDEEN GOLF CLUB – BALGOWNIE LINKS

Royal Aberdeen Golf Club,
Links Road,
Bridge Of Don,
Aberdeen,
AB23 8AT
**www.royalaberdeengolf.com**
**Phone:** +44 (0) 1224 702571
**Email:** admin@royalaberdeengolf.com

**Essential course details –**
**Par:** 71 (White tees) / 73 (Green tees)
**S.S.S:** 73 (White tees) / 72 (Green tees)
**Slope:** 144 (White tees) / 133 (Green tees)
**Length:** 5,199yds–6,537yds
**Longest hole:** Par-5 2nd, 427yds–567yds
**Shortest hole:** Par-3 8th, 133yds–147yds
**Type:** Links

**Handicap Certificate:** Required (maximum of 24 for both men and ladies)

**Green fees:**
▼ per round (high season)
▼ full day
▼ per round (low season)
Juniors – 50 per cent of adult prices

**Caddies:**
£50 (+ gratuity). Booked in advance upon request.

**Equipment hire:**
£45 – club hire
£15 – electric trolley
£6 – pull trolley

**How do I book a round of golf?**
Royal Aberdeen Golf Club is a private members club; however, visitor bookings are available for the Balgownie Links course on the following times during the week:

**Monday & Wednesday**
10.00 am–11.30 am & 2.00 pm–3.30 pm
Tuesday & Thursday
2.00 pm–3.30 pm
Friday
10.00 am–11.00 am & 2.30 pm–3.30 pm

**Weekends**
after 3.30 pm

There are two ways to book a round of golf at Royal Aberdeen Golf Club:

*Phone:*
+44 (0) 1224 702571

*Email:*
reservations@royalaberdeengolf.com (include all relevant details – preferred dates/times, group size etc)
　　Email reservations can also be reached via the club website. A 25 per cent non-refundable deposit is required on confirmation of the booking and the balance paid in full one month before play.

**Looking down the fairway of the 4th hole, regarded as the toughest on the Balgownie Links Course.**
*Royal Aberdeen Golf Club.*

## HISTORY

Aberdeen has a golf tradition stretching back much further than its oldest club. In 1538 and 1545, there are references to 'goiff' and 'goiff ballis' in Aberdeen City Records. The earliest reference in Scotland to golf holes is believed to be here in 1625, when a local Aberdeen record discusses some military exercises 'in the principal parts of the links betwixt the first hole and the Quenis [sic] hole.' (Source: www.scottishgolfhistory.org)

Founded in 1780, Royal Aberdeen is reputedly the sixth oldest golf club in the world. For the first thirty-five years of its existence the club was known as The Society of Golfers at Aberdeen. On the 1 June 1815, on the eve of the Battle of Waterloo, the society changed its name to The Aberdeen Golf Club. In 1872 the club received the patronage of Prince Leopold. However, the royal title was not applied for until 1903 and granted by King Edward VII on 10 August that year.

Since 1827 club members have worn distinctive red jackets (they were originally green but this colour proved unpopular). The club originally played its golf on the local Queens Links, however, this course became too crowded, so in 1888 the club moved to Balgownie links. The course was originally designed by Archie and Robert Simpson and received a re-design in 1925 by James Braid. More recently, from the year 2000, it has been sympathetically modified and improved by Dr Martin Hawtree.

In recent years the course has hosted the 2005 British Senior Open, 2011 Walker Cup and the 2014 Scottish Open – the first major European tour event in the club's history.

## PLAYING THE COURSE

The Balgownie links is a traditional out and back course running alongside the North Sea. The outward 9 holes are regarded as among the best Scotland has to offer. Hole 1 takes you out towards the shoreline while the next 8 holes all run parallel along the coast. The front-9, from the tee-boxes, appear quite narrow with dunes flanking each side of the fairway. Placement really is key, therefore, keep checking your guide for distances as a ball into the long

**17** **SIGNATURE HOLE: PAR-3 8TH 147YDS.**
The main difference between this and the previous holes – this is the first hole you'll play with the wind coming straight at you rather than behind. Club selection can be a nightmare. You may need a 3-iron one day, pitching wedge the next. Nine bunkers surround the green like dragon's teeth and the only way home is straight down its throat.

**The 8th green guarded by bunkers.**
*Credit: Royal Aberdeen Golf Club.*

**A tricky approach towards the 12th green with bunkers both left and right.** *Royal Aberdeen Golf Club.*

grass on the dunes offers absolutely no bailout scenario. There is very little requirement for a driver on this course with most holes presenting a slight advantage to the right of the fairway.

The back-9 bring you back to the clubhouse and are more elevated than the front, with stunning views out to sea. Many members would argue that the back-9 are actually tougher than the front-9 as they're more exposed to the elements.

After a testing par-4 1st, the 2nd hole is the longest hole on the course – 567yds, par-5. After a long carry over a hill the fairway is protected either side by a valley of sand dunes. The approach shot can be hit low to avoid the wind. Hole 3 is a 218-yard par-3 on an elevated tee. Aim to the right of the green, if short, the ball can be gathered up by the slope and carried down to the putting surface. A par here is a very good score.

Holes 4 and 5 are tough par-4s requiring accuracy from the tee and straight drives. Hole 6 is a relatively short par-5 with a bottleneck into the green so either go long or lay up short for a chip up towards the green.

The back-9 will seem different in appearance and nature from the seaward holes but every bit the stalwart test. Less undulating than the front-9, the remaining holes use blind tee-shots, hidden troughs and more difficult putting surfaces to challenge you. On the 10th, drive over the correct marker poles – coloured according to the tee you are on. Depending on wind direction a driver may not be necessary here and a good tee-shot should leave you with a mid to short iron into a green that slopes from back to front.

The 13th is aptly named 'Blind' due to its blind tee-shot, and sometimes your second. Here, the best line is to hug the right side. A long drive that carries the hill will find a fairway that slopes and kicks the ball forward. The 2nd shot is awkward as the green is narrow front to back. Don't miss this green, as there's trouble behind.

The concluding three holes form an excellent 4-3-4 finish. The 16th plays to the top of the hill giving a view of the green. Otherwise it's another blind 2nd shot favouring the right-hand side. If you clear the crest it's 160yds to the front edge of a fast green that slopes front to back quite severely. Hole 17 is a par-3 facing the sea where your tee-shot has to battle, at times, severe cross-winds towards a three-tiered green.

In terms of disguised difficulty, there are few that can top Balgownie's 18th. Most members play it as a par-5. It is usually into the wind, but you need to avoid the fairway bunkers running left and right. The green is slightly raised and well protected with bunkers and out of bounds at the back. This ensures that you must remain as focused as you were on the first tee if you are to find this green in two.

# Other courses on site

In addition to the Balgownie Links course, Royal Aberdeen Golf Club also has the following course available for visitors to play:

● **SILVERBURN COURSE (18 HOLES)**
A short 18 holes ideal for beginners with nine par-3's and a mixture of both parkland and links background.

**Par:** 64
**Length:** 4,021yds
**Green Fees:**
▼ adult & juniors per round

# 18-hole courses nearby

## ● MURCAR LINKS

Established in 1909 and right next door to Royal Aberdeen. A beautiful links course originally designed by Archie Simpson and revised in the 1930s by James Braid. A natural championship course and a real test, in particular if the wind is swirling.

**Website:** www.murcarlinks.com
**Email:** golf@murcarlinks.com
**Telephone:** +44 (0) 1224 704354

**Par:** 68 (White tees) / 72 (Blue tees)
**Length:** 5,577yds–6,303yds
**Type:** Links
**Fees:**
▼ per round (weekdays & weekend)

**Visitor Tee Times:**
Available seven days a week, however, check the visitor section on the website as each day has different times.

## ● STONEHAVEN

Overlooking the North Sea and the harbour town of Stonehaven. Not the longest course in the world but, without doubt, a unique setting, with some of the most dramatic holes in the area, right on the cliff top.

**Website:** www.stonehavengolfclub.com
**Email:** N/A
**Telephone:** +44 (0) 1569 762124

**Par:** 66 (White tees) / 67 (Red tees)
**Length:** 4,572yds–5,103yds
**Type:** Links

**Fees:**
▼ per round (weekdays & weekend)

## ● KINGS LINKS

An old school links course under the stewardship of the city council. Running right along the beach front with big dunes, fast greens and lots of bunkers.

**Website:** www.sportaberdeen.co.uk
**Email:** golf@sportaberdeen.co.uk
**Telephone:** +44 (0) 1224 507767

**Par:** 71
**Length:** 6,289yds
**Type:** Municipal Links

**Fees:**
▼ per round (weekdays & weekend)

## ROYAL DORNOCH GOLF CLUB – CHAMPIONSHIP COURSE

Royal Dornoch Golf Club,
Golf Rd,
Dornoch,
IV25 3LW
**www.royaldornoch.com**
**Phone:** +44 (0) 1862 810219
**Email:** bookings@royaldornoch.com

Essential course details –
**Par:** 70 (Blue tees) / 76 (Green tees)
**SSS:** 73 (Blue tees) / 76 (Green tees)
**Slope rating:** 136 (Blue tees) / 130 (Green tees)
**Length:** 5,359yds–6,748yds
**Longest hole:** Par-5 12th, 453yds–560yds
**Shortest hole:** Par-3 6th, 125yds–161yds
**Type:** Links

**Handicap Certificate:** Not required The official club website advises golfers with a handicap of 24 or below for men and 30 or below for ladies would be most suited to the Championship Course.

**Green fees:**
▼ per round (high season)
▼ per round (low season)
▽ day ticket (high season)
▽ day ticket (low season)
▽ combination ticket* (high season)
▽ combination ticket* (low season)
▽ twilight ticket**

* = One round on Championship Course and one on Struie Course on the same day OR over two consecutive days
** = Twilight times – May–July, 6.00 pm / August, 5.30 pm

**Caddies:**
£50 per player (+ gratuity)
£30 junior caddie (+ gratuity)
Forecaddies available on request.

**Equipment hire:**
Clubs and push trollies are available upon request. Buggies are only available for medical reasons.

**How do I book a round of golf?**
Royal Dornoch is a private members club; however, visitors are welcome to play seven days a week subject to availability.

There are three ways to book a round of golf for the Championship Course at Royal Dornoch:

*Online:*
www.royaldornoch.com/play/book

*Phone:*
+44 (0) 1862 810219

*Email:*
bookings@royaldornoch.com (include all relevant details – preferred dates/times, group size etc)

## HISTORY

Early golf on Dornoch links can be traced as far back as 1616 where there is a record of £10 being spent on golfing equipment for the young Earl of Sutherland. His tutor, Sir Robert Gordon of Gordonstoun, would state in 1628 that the links of Dornoch were the 'fairest and lairgist links of any part of Scotland'. (Source: www.scottishgolfhistory.org)

The Championship course dates back to 1877 when the Dornoch Golf Club was founded, initially, with just 9 holes. In 1886, Old Tom Morris laid out the remaining course. Morris would later take on an apprentice called Donald Ross who, in 1899, would leave Scotland for America where he became one of the most respected course architects of his time, responsible for the design of some of the most famous courses on the US circuit including Pinehurst No 2 and Oakland Hills.

In 1906, through the influence of Her Grace the Duchess of Sutherland, Duchess Millicent, a good friend to the Club, Dornoch Golf Club secured the title and dignity of 'Royal' from King Edward VII.

**View of the Clubhouse and the course stretching along the curving bay of Dornoch Firth.**
*Royal Dornoch Golf Club.*

In the aftermath of the Second World War further changes were made to the course under the guidance of George Duncan and Robbie Grant the head greenkeeper at the time. The new holes form the present 6th to 11th loop, incorporating the features introduced by Old Tom Morris with the new layout ready for play in 1948.

## PLAYING THE COURSE

The Championship Course is something of an enigma in that it's not at all deceptive. There are precious few blind shots or hidden bunkers to contend with. In fact, virtually all of the hazards are clearly visible. That's the good news and also the bad news because seeing a hazard in front of you doesn't make it any less intimidating.

Unlike many links golf courses where a bump and run will bring you closer to the pin than a high pitch shot, the greens on this course are protected by bunkers at the front of the green and/or are set on a plateaux so that a bump and run has to be perfectly executed.

The Championship Course is a classic out-and-back links golf course but with a twist – an 'S' shaped twist. When playing the usual out-and-back layouts you have to contend with the wind blowing in only two directions – one way when you're going out and the opposite way when coming back. This course, however, is laid out in more of an 'S' shape, which means that no matter which way the wind is blowing, on every hole it will be blowing in a different direction.

The 1st hole is a gentle start, 331-yard par-4. Nevertheless, there are nine bunkers to negotiate and plenty of gorse lining the fairway. Hole 2 is a par-3 that plays only 184yds, but you could be hitting anything from a 3 wood to a wedge depending on the wind. The green is an 'inverted saucer', any shot not landing and holding the green rolls off leaving a tough recovery shot. Take note of the inverted saucer green because you'll see it throughout this course.

**The 4th green sits above the fairway.** *Royal Dornoch Golf Club.*

**The 5th green protected by three bunkers with the 6th green in the distance, below a blanket of yellow gorse on the hillside.** *Royal Dornoch Golf Club.*

It not only makes for a difficult approach shot, it makes the greens seem smaller than they are, again adding to the intimidation factor. A well-struck shot that is able to hold the green or a well-judged shot that rolls up and stops will serve you well on this course.

Holes 4 and 5 are both equally demanding par-4s. The tee-shot from the 5th is around 40ft above the fairway that slopes fiercely down to a green with three bunkers guarding the front to make any attempted bump and run a little more daunting. There's no easy way on to the green other than dead centre.

The fun continues at the par-3 6th, at 163 yards it doesn't appear to offer too much of a challenge, but the tee-shot is to a raised green built into a

**The approach from the ridge towards the 8th green. The next ten holes head back towards the Clubhouse.** *Royal Dornoch Golf Club.*

The ridge on the 17th fairway before the hole doglegs left towards the green. *Royal Dornoch Golf Club.*

gorse-covered hillside. Anything too far left is in deep gorse, anything too far right will fall back down the side or into a deep bunker. On it goes, hole after hole. You can see what's coming – there is nothing hidden – and the right shot to make, but you can also see what any mistakes will bring. The bunkers are deep and can require your hitting the ball backwards or sideways onto the fairway rather than playing it toward the green.

**(14) SIGNATURE HOLE: PAR-4 14TH, 401-445YDS, 'FOXY'.**
The only hole without a bunker – it doesn't need one. A double dogleg fairway guarded on both sides by grassy ridges that manage to jut out far enough to catch any wayward drive. If you hit a great drive then go for the pin, but this is a narrow green, again on a plateau, so you'll need to be accurate with any approach shot. Playing to your handicap on this hole is something to cherish.

# Other courses on site

In addition to the Championship Course, Royal Dornoch also has the following course available for visitors to play:

● **STRUIE COURSE (18 HOLES)**
Royal Dornoch has a special place in many golfers hearts, and not just because of the Championship Course. The Struie originally opened as a 12-hole ladies course in 1899 and 100 years later was finally upgraded to 18 holes. The journey to Dornoch can be a long one – make sure you take advantage of both courses during your visit.

**Par:** 71 (White tees) / 72 (Red tees)
**S.S.S:** 70 (White tees) / 72 (Red tees)
**Length:** 5,211yds–6,265yds

**Green fees:**
▼ per round
▼: twilight ticket (times as stated on page 108)

# 18-hole courses nearby

### ● BRORA GOLF CLUB

Established in 1891, the most northerly of all James Braid's designs and also the headquarters of the James Braid Golfing Society. Rolling fairways, colourful gorse, burn water, a beach running alongside and even a nearby railway. Just sixteen miles north of Dornoch, you should make time to enjoy a round at Brora.

**Website:** www.broragolfclub.co.uk
**Email:** secretary@broragolfclub.co.uk
**Telephone:** +44 (0) 1408 621417

**Par:** 70 (White tees) / 71 (Red tees)
**Length:** 5,273yds–6,211yds
**Type:** Links

**Fees:**
▼ per round (Monday–Sunday)

### ● GOLSPIE GOLF CLUB

Approximately 15 miles north of Dornoch, this James Braid designed course offers an intriguing mix of classic links and parkland holes with the Dornoch Firth on one side and the backdrop of Ben Bhraggie on the other.

**Website**: www.golspiegolfclub.co.uk
**Email:** info@golspiegolfclub.co.uk
**Telephone:** +44 (0) 1408 633266

**Par:** 70 (White tees) / 72 (Red tees)
**Length:** 5,238yds–6,021yds
**Type:** Links

**Fees:**
▼ per round (weekday & weekend) (Discount green fee available for members of James Braid courses)

### ● TAIN GOLF CLUB

Nine miles south of Dornoch and regarded as Old Tom Morris' northern jewel. Sea on one side and the mountain backdrop on the other, this course presents a truly original challenge to golfers of all levels and abilities.

**Website:** www.tain-golfclub.co.uk
**Email:** info@tain-golfclub.co.uk
**Telephone:** +44 (0) 1862 892314

**Par:** 70 (White tees) / 73 (Red tees)
**Length:** 5,645yds–6,404yds
**Type:** Links

**Fees:**
▼ per round (weekday & weekend) Twilight rates apply (after 4 pm May/ June/July)

## ROYAL TROON GOLF CLUB – OLD COURSE

Royal Troon Golf Club
Craigend Road
Troon
KA10 6EP
**www.royaltroon.co.uk**
**Phone:** +44 (0) 1292 311 555
**Email:** admin@royaltroon.com

**Essential course details –**
**Par:** 71 (White tees) / 75 (Red tees)
**S.S.S:** 73 (White tees) / 76 (Red tees)
**Slope rating:** 136 (White tees) / 134 (Red tees)
**Length:** 6,108yds–6,632yds
**Longest hole:** Par-5 6th, 508yds–544yds
**Shortest hole:** Par-3 8th, 118yds–123yds
**Type:** Links

**Handicap Certificate:** Required
(maximum 20 handicap for men, 30
for ladies)

### Green fees:
▼ per round
▼ PGA Member

### Caddies:
£50 per round, per golfer. (+gratuity).
Must be booked in advance.

### Equipment hire:
£50 – clubs, per round
£20 – electric trolley
£7.50 – pull trolley

### How do I book a round of golf?
Royal Troon is a private members Golf
Club; however, it welcomes visitors
every Monday, Tuesday and Thursday
between late April and October every
year. Visitors may be asked to bring
their handicap certificates on the day
of their round.

There are three ways to book a
round of golf for the Old Course at
Royal Troon:

*Online:*
www.royaltroon.co.uk/visitors/book-
online

*Phone:*
+44 (0) 1292 311555

*Email:*
bookings@royaltroon.com (include
all relevant details – preferred dates/
times, group size etc)

### HISTORY
Troon Golf Club was formed on
16 March 1878, at a meeting of
enthusiasts in a local hostelry – The
Portland Arms Hotel. The Club's first
Honorary President was His Grace
William John Arthur Charles James
who was The 6th Duke of Portland.
The duke owned the local links
land where the course was to be
constructed and he took an active

**The 18th green at the Old Course with the Clubhouse behind.** *Royal Troon Golf Club.*

interest in promoting this development as a valuable local attraction.

Initially the course had just 5 holes but by 1885 it had undergone a series of redevelopments and expanded up to 18. The 1882 Open Champion, Willie Fernie, orchestrated the original design alongside the club's first appointed professional, George Strath. Fernie would take over as head professional in 1887 and would remain in that position until his death in 1924.

In 1923, prior to Fernie's death, the course would undergo a significant re-design ahead of hosting its first Open Championship. This time the changes were coordinated by James Braid and have remained broadly untouched through to its current layout.

The Open Championship has been held at the Old Course nine times, most recently in 2016 with Henrik Stenson emerging victorious – the first European to do so at this course since Arthur Havers way back in 1923.

The course holds the distinction of having the shortest (Postage Stamp, 8th) and longest (Turnberry, 6th) hole on The Open roster. In 1962, 22-year-old Jack Nicklaus took his Open bow at Troon having just won the US Open a few weeks prior. He would finish a lowly tied 34th.

The club also holds in its possession (reputedly) the oldest set of clubs known in existence – the Adam Wood Clubs. Expressed opinions maintain the clubs date back circa 600 years and belonged to the time of the Stuart Kings.

## PLAYING THE COURSE

The Old Course is a traditional links layout with the first 9 holes moving away from the clubhouse and the back-9 heading towards it. The perceived wisdom states the front nine are the most picturesque as they stretch along the coastline and are the most enjoyable to play. It is here that you can soak up the views, on a clear day, of Ailsa Craig towards the south and the Isle Of Arran in the west.

The first three holes, all par-4s less than 400yds, are a fairly straightforward start. The 2nd and 3rd holes both offer fairway hazards off the tee – the 2nd with three bunkers at around 250yds and a burn on the 3rd at 280yds. Most mid-level handicappers should roll their ball up rather than try anything clever. The greens all offer plenty of space to aim for.

The first real test comes at the par-5 4th, a long dogleg right with a bunker on the right of the fairway at 250yds to carry. A two-tier green provides a tough finish. Be very happy with a handicap score here. The first par-3 follows with 209yds and 195yds to the front, it's a long one. Bunkers await anything short, so take an extra club if you feel you need it to carry up to the green.

The 7th is a favourite hole for many on the course – stunning views and a challenging dogleg right par-4 with lots and lots of bunkers. Then it's on to another **signature hole – the par-3 'Postage Stamp'**; 123yds, elevated tee, a downhill short green surrounded by bunkers. What's not to like? Those who are adamant a par-3 less than 150yds cannot be challenging somehow miss what makes golf so enjoyable.

After a par-4 9th it's the long stretch home. The 10th doesn't ease you in like the 1st – a blind tee-shot over sandhills. The 11th – 'Railway' hole is another scary tee-shot with 200yds of gorse to pass before hitting the fairway.

**6** **SIGNATURE HOLE: PAR-5 6TH, 508–544YDS, 'TURNBERRY'.**
Bunkers are waiting for you at 277yds off the tee on this monster hole. If, like most, you're going at the green in three shots – be wary of the pot bunkers 50yds out from the green. An accurate short game is needed if you're going to get anywhere near a handicap score on this hole. Aim right when going for the green as a bunker sits short-left.

View from behind the green at the long par-5 6th, 'Turnberry'. *Royal Troon Golf Club.*

**View from the tee towards the green at the famous par-3 Postage Stamp.** *Royal Troon Golf Club.*

Anything too far right on this hole is dicing with railway lines and oncoming trains. The 12th and 13th are both long par-4s – and expect both of them to play long.

The last 6 holes all play directly into the wind as you head straight towards the clubhouse. Accuracy here is crucial as you either face strategically placed bunkers or heavy gorse as you traverse your way home. The 17th is the longest par-3 at 220yds, five bunkers surround the green all waiting for your ball to fall short.

And finally it's on to the 18th. The fairway bunker on the right that trapped Greg Norman in 1989 sits at around 310yds; aim straight for it from the tee. Hitting into the wind, the likelihood is your ball will not find it as Norman's did. This offers you the better line for your second shot. The green, again, has five pot bunkers surrounding it. Anything long can be out of bounds so, for one last swing on this legendary course, make it dead centre.

**Looking down the fairway from the green towards the railway line at the 12th hole.** *Royal Troon Golf Club.*

# Other courses on site

In addition to the Old Course, Royal Troon Golf Club also has the following course available for visitors to play:

● **PORTLAND COURSE (18 HOLES)**
Opened in 1895 and re-designed by Dr Alister MacKenzie in the early 1920s. The Portland Course is more sheltered from the shoreline and offers an interesting layout with five par-3s and five par-5s – four on the back-9 – on the scorecard. Same rules apply for visitor days and methods of booking as the Old Course.

**Par:** 72 (White tees) / 75 (Red tees)
**S.S.S:** 71 (White tees) / 75 (Red tees)
**Length:** 5,811yds–6,349yds

**Green fees:**
▼ per round
▼ PGA member

# 18-hole courses nearby

● **THE IRVINE GOLF CLUB**
Established in 1887, the course at Irvine Golf Club is considered one of Scotland's hidden gems and one of the best rounds of golf for less than £100 anywhere in the land. The course was re-designed by James Braid in 1926 and is a traditional links challenge with many features laid down by Braid still present today.

**Website:** www.theirvinegolfclub.co.uk
**Email:** secretary@theirvinegolfclub.co.uk
**Telephone:** +44 (0) 1294 275979

**Par:** 70 (Yellow tees) / 72 (Red tees)
**Length:** 5,661yds–6,116yds
**Type:** Links

**Fees:**
▼ per round (weekday & weekend)

**19**

# SOUTHERNESS GOLF CLUB

Southerness Golf Club,
Southerness,
Dumfries,
DG2 8AZ
**www.southernessgolfclub.com**
**Phone:** +44 (0) 1387 880677
**Email:** southernessgc@btconnect.com

**Essential course details –**
**Par:** 69 (White tees) / 73 (Red tees)
**S.S.S:** 73 (White tees) / 73 (Red tees)
**Length:** 5,622yds–6,566yds
**Longest hole:** Par-5 5th, 433yds–496yds
**Shortest hole:** Par-3 10th, 141yds–168yds
**Type:** Links

**Handicap Certificate:** Required
(maximum 28 for men and 36 for
ladies)

**Green fees:**
▼ per round (weekdays & weekends)
▼ per day (weekdays & weekends)
▼ juniors (10–17 years)

**Caddies:**
Available upon request only

**Equipment hire:**
Clubs/trolleys available on the day
from the pro-shop

**How do I book a round of golf?**
Southerness Golf Club is a private
members club; however, visitor

bookings are available for the
following times during the week –

Mon / Tues / Wed / Fri
10.00 am–12.00 pm & 2.00 pm–4.00 pm
Thursday 11.00 am–12.00 pm & 2.30
    pm–4.00 pm
Saturday / Sunday 10.00 am–12.00 pm
    & 2.00 pm–4.00 pm
There are three ways to book a round
of golf at Southerness Golf Club:

*Online:*
www.southernessgolfclub.com – go to
visitors page for booking link

*Phone:*
+44 (0) 1387 880677

*Email:*
southernessgc@btconnect.com
(include all relevant details –
preferred dates/times, group size etc)

## HISTORY
Southerness Lighthouse has been a
prominent landmark for the coastal
town of Southerness since 1748,
making it the second oldest surviving
lighthouse in Scotland. Altered and
eventually left derelict in 1867, the
lighthouse was restored in 1894 and
heightened to 17 metres. It remained
in active service until 1936 and has
become the emblem of Southerness
Golf Club.

The Oswald family have been intertwined with the history of Southerness since its development from a small mining village and depot for coal. Major Richard Oswald, descendant from the Oswald clan, was born and served in India during the Second World War with the Bengal Lancers. He eventually returned to Scotland to oversee military training.

After the end of the war, in 1946, Major Oswald decided to give the town of Southerness the one thing it was missing – a links golf course. Originally the course measured 6,250yds, however, tiger tees were available which increased the length to over 7,000yds. The course was completed for the princely sum of £2,000.

Sea erosion has been a constant issue for the club to deal with; however, with a passionate membership and strong leadership over the years, the club have dealt with this and seen the growth of the clubhouse along with changes to the course, making it a true championship links layout.

## PLAYING THE COURSE

Southerness, as its name suggests, is the most southerly point in Scotland where you can play a course of this quality. You could be forgiven for looking at the total yardage and thinking this may not be the toughest challenge. However, the overall par of 69 more than makes up for this and with a standard scratch score of 73, a round of golf here can prove to be a vigorous test.

Two short par-5s are where birdie opportunities are to be found, but eight par-4s over 400yds are where shots can be dropped. The fairways appear quite inviting and generous, but the surrounding rough will gobble up any wayward shots. The driver is definitely needed on this course so you'll need to keep focus and aim straight. Southerness is an easy walking course with no hills or difficult terrain to negotiate so just relax and enjoy your round.

**The two-tiered green at the par-3 4th, the first of five par-3s at Southerness.** *Southerness Golf Club.*

The 12th green offers incredible views looking out towards the Solway Firth. *Southerness Golf Club.*

## 12 SIGNATURE HOLE: PAR-4 12TH, 365–421YDS.

The most memorable hole on the course, with terrific views of the Solway Firth right ahead as you stand on the tee. Fairway bunkers both right and left await anything off line so don't let the view distract you. Bunkers on the right, a pond on the left and the sandy bay off the back protect the green.

The 1st hole is a par-4 with a slight dogleg left to right. A fence running along the right represents out of bounds so best to avoid this. Missing the fairway will introduce you to the abundance of heather in evidence all around the course. Hole 2 is the first of the 400+yds par-4s and another dogleg left to right. It's also played into the prevailing wind so, overall, a tough two shots to the green.

After another long par-4, the 4th hole is the first par-3. Bunkers wait at the front and right for anything off target. The 5th is a fairly short par-5, but with an elevated green it makes any approach shot a tricky one. The 7th is a long par-3 where you catch your first sight of the Solway Firth. Holes 8 & 9 are par-4s before the second par-3 at the 10th as you turn form home. This hole is all carry with the green surrounded by seven bunkers.

The 13th is a formidable hole – 467-yard, par-4. Fairway bunkers reside on the left and semi-rough on the right. Playing to your handicap here should definitely put a smile on your face. The final three holes give you a trio of par variety. The 16th is the final long par-4 before the final par-3 at hole 17. The good news is there are no bunkers at the 17th, but it is an elevated green so your tee-shot needs to be solid if it's to hold its place.

Your round finishes with a par-5. Long hitters can make the green in two but will need to be accurate both from the tee and with the approach. Bunkers sit 60yds from the green, ready to catch anything short.

# 18-hole courses nearby

## ● DUMFRIES AND GALLOWAY GOLF CLUB

Visitors are welcome all through the week and weekends at this exquisite championship parkland course.

**Website:** www.dandggolfclub.co.uk
**Email:** info@dandggolfclub.co.uk
**Telephone:** +44 (0) 1387 263848

**Par:** 70 (White tees) / 72 (Red tees)
**Length:** 5,328yds–6,222yds
**Type:** Parkland

**Fees:**
▼ per round (weekdays & weekends)

## ● DUMFRIES AND COUNTY GOLF CLUB

Opened in 1913 and originally designed by Willie Fernie, this challenging parkland course was re-designed by James Braid in 1929.

**Website:** www.thecounty.co.uk
**Email:** admin@thecounty.co.uk
**Telephone:** +44 (0) 1387 253585

**Par:** 69 (White tees) / 72 (Red tees)
**Length:** 5,420yds–5,925yds
**Type:** Parkland

**Fees:**
▼ per round (weekdays & weekends)

## ● COLVEND GOLF CLUB

Just a short drive along the Solway coast from Southerness, tree-lined fairways are in abundance at this beautiful parkland course. Originally built by Willie Fernie, more recently the course has been re-designed by among others, Peter Alliss.

**Website:** www.colvendgolfclub.co.uk
**Email:** secretary@colvendgolfclub.co.uk
**Telephone:** +44 (0) 1556 630398

**Par:** 69 (White tees) / 70 (Red tees)
**Length:** 4,774yds–5,341yds
**Type:** Parkland

**Fees:**
▼ per round (weekdays & weekends)

## ● POWFOOT GOLF CLUB

A delightful, scenic course opened in 1903 and re-designed by James Braid in 1923, offering an intriguing mixture of links and parkland golf.

**Website:** www.powfootgolfclub.com
**Email:** info@powfootgolfclub.com
**Telephone:** +44 (0) 1461 204100

**Par:** 71 (White tees) / 74 (Red tees)
Length: 5,489yds–6,274yds
Type: Links/Parkland

**Fees:**
▼ per round (weekdays & weekends)

**20**

## ST ANDREWS – OLD COURSE
Links Clubhouse,
West Sands,
St Andrews,
KY16 9XL
**www.standrews.com**
**Phone:** +44 (0) 1334 466 718
(Reservations)
+44 (0) 1334 466 666 (Reception)
**Email:** reservations@standrews.com

**Essential course details –**
**Par:** 72 (White tees) / 76 (Red tees)
**S.S.S:** 73 (White tees) / 76 (Red tees)
**Slope:** 132 (White tees) / 138 (Red tees)
**Length:** 6,032yds–6,721yds
**Longest hole:** Par-5 14th, 487yds–530yds
**Shortest hole:** Par-3 8th, 145yds–166yds
**Type:** Links

**Handicap Certificate:** Required
(maximum handicap is 24 for men
and 36 for ladies)

**Green fees:**
▼ per round (low season)
▼ per round (shoulder season)
▼ per round (high season)

**Caddies:**
£55 per round, £35 for a trainee caddie
(+gratuity). Must book in advance.

**Equipment hire:**
£35 – clubs

£20 – electric trolley
£5 – push trolley
Buggies can be requested for the
Old Course by anyone registered
disabled. They're available April to
October only and driven by a qualified
caddie driver. The buggy is provided
free but the caddie fee is payable.

**How do I book a round of golf?**
St Andrews is open to the general
public, however, the Old Course
attracts 45,000 rounds of golf a year,
therefore, special conditions apply to
booking a tee-time.

**Advanced reservation** – contact
the reservation department directly by
telephone (+44 (0) 1334 466718) or by
email (reservations@standrews.com).

**Public Ballot** – around 50 per cent
of the course's availability is drawn
by public ballot, which is announced
two days in advance. So, for example,
tee-times for 22 June are drawn on
20 June and so on. The Old Course is
closed for golf on Sundays so there
is no ballot held on Fridays. Entering
the ballot is no guarantee that you
will receive a tee-time. A minimum
of two golfers can enter the ballot
either by telephone, online, or in
person before 2 pm and two days
before play. Those who secure a tee
time can find out after 4 pm on the
course website, at the clubhouse,
the starters box, the caddie pavilion

or the St Andrews Visit Scotland Information Centre.

**Single Golfers** – if you're flying solo you can check in directly at the Old Pavilion on the day (get there early) and you can get paired with a two or three-ball group. The group is not obliged to agree to it, but general golf etiquette dictates that you will be welcome to join.

## HISTORY

The home of golf can trace its origins back as far as the early fifteenth century. In 1552 Archbishop John Hamilton allowed the townsfolk of St Andrews the right to play on the links. In 1754 a group of twenty-two landowners founded the Society of St Andrews Golfers, a precursor to the Royal & Ancient governing body that controls the modern-day global game outside the US and Mexico.

In 1921 Bobby Jones made his first appearance at the Old Course in The Open Championship. Halfway through his third round he walked off the course having suffered the indignity of taking four swings at his ball, which was plugged in a bunker at the 11th hole, still unable to get it out. Six years later Jones returned and would claim a stunning six-shot victory, having led wire-to-wire, and claim The Open Championship for the second time. Jones would go on to co-found The Masters Tournament at Augusta National but he would also claim to be in love with the Old Course for the rest of his life.

**One of the most famous sites in golf. Looking towards the 18th green and 1st tee at the Old Course, St Andrews.** *St Andrews Links.*

## PLAYING THE COURSE

Ken Brown, former pro and now BBC commentator, once said (with tongue firmly in cheek) that the first time you play the Old Course you'll probably hate it. One of the issues you face is a sense of familiarity. We all feel like it's a course we know well because we've seen it – and dreamt about playing it – so many times. But watching the professionals go to work during an Open Championship and making those shots ourselves are two very different things.

President Eisenhower was so nervous when he arrived at the 1st tee he decided to skip the hole altogether and went straight to the 2nd. So, if you feel some of the same jitters – don't worry, you're in good company.

Adding to the drama are the crowds that flock to the home of golf, in particular during the summer. If you secure a round during the high season expect to have between fifty and a hundred spectators milling around the 1st tee and 18th green as you prepare to make that daunting first swing. Just remember, as with their heroes who tee-up during The Open, they're all routing for you so take a deep breath and give your ball a good whack.

The Old Course is as traditional as it gets with the course starting and finishing back in town. A general rule, both going out and coming back, the further left you are off the tee, the safer it is, but harder from there to get close to the pins. So, the more right you are the bigger risk you take of going out of bounds but if you get it right then you're left with a better angle into the flag.

**17** **SIGNATURE HOLE: PAR-4 17TH, 426–455YD, 'ROAD'.**

The iconic road hole is simply known as 'Road' on the Old Course scorecard. One of the toughest par-4 holes in golf starts with an unsighted tee-shot over the corner of the hotel sheds. As you prepare to take your tee-shot you will see the sheds adorned with the hotel logo and the words – 'Old Course Hotel'. The perceived wisdom for the perfect line, if you're confident with the distance, is to aim for the 'H'. The longer you can drive the ball determines how far right along the letters you should aim for. If you're really confident or your name's Dustin Johnson go for the 'l'.

If you decide to go for the green and end up in the infamous bunker then take comfort in knowing the best golfers the world has ever seen have shared your pain. If you fly over the green and end up on the road there is no relief and that is where you must play it.

There are 112 bunkers across the course; only the 1st and 18th holes have none at all. Part of the aura of the course stems from the fact a lot of the bunkers are unsighted from the tee. Some of the names of these traps, such as 'Hell' and 'The Coffins', are designed to invoke fear before you even reach them. The Coffins lies at driving distance on the testing par-4 13th. A visit here is effectively a penalty shot.

If you manage to make it to the greens avoiding sand, the huge putting surfaces (14 holes are shared double greens) present their own problems with plenty of 40ft putts making you sweat for your par.

So, a very stimulating, tactical, challenge and that's without any wind. It can differ in strength and direction constantly. It can be downwind on the front-9 and upwind on the backward stretch or vice versa. But remember, a true test of any links course is not complete without an unpredictable wind.

And finally there's the history. As you approach the 18th tee and see the Swilcan Bridge, with the green sat in the shadow of the R&A Golf Club in the distance, you stand on the shoulders of giants. This is where Bobby Jones, Nicklaus, Faldo, Seve and Tiger all stood to make their final big swing before being crowned Champion Golfer. The Old Course is a sacred place, steeped in legend. St Andrews is unique and a round of golf here will stay with you for the rest of your life.

**The infamous Hell Bunker lurks on the long, par-5, 14th fairway. Avoid at all costs.** *St Andrews Links.*

# Other courses on site

The Old Course is one, albeit incredibly important, part of St Andrews Links. In addition there are a further six courses available for visitors to play:

The Castle Course offers incredible views of the historic town of St Andrews. *St Andrews Links.*

### ● THE CASTLE COURSE (18 HOLES)

The newest addition to the St Andrews stable of fine courses. Opened in 2008 and described as golfing on the edge of paradise, with the course perched on a cliff-top offering incredible views over St Andrews.

The Castle Course is typically closed during low season, usually reopening at the beginning of March until the beginning of November. Expect to use fairway mats until the beginning of April.

Online bookings can be made up to two days in advance of play with the full green fee payable. Within two days bookings must be made via telephone (+44 (0) 1334 466666) and payment taken on the day at the clubhouse before play commences.

You can also call the reservations department on +44 (0) 1334 466718.

**Par:** 71 (White tees) / 71 (Red tees)
**Length:** 5,460yds–6,759yds
**Type:** Links

**Green fees:**
▼ adult per round (March/Shoulder season)
▼ adult per round (High Season)
▼ junior per round (March/Shoulder/High season)

### ● NEW COURSE (18 HOLES)

Designed by Tom Morris in 1895, named in order to make the strikingly obvious statement of differentiating it from its illustrious older brother. The New Course is described as the oldest new course in the world. Considered a

Despite its name, the New Course at St Andrews is over 120 years old. *St Andrews Links.*

strong test of links golf in its own right.

Bookings can be made either online or via the reservations department (+44 (0) 1334 466718) up to two days in advance. You can book within two days by approaching the starter on the day of play who will allocate available tee-times on a first come first served basis. Full payment is made direct to the starter.

**Par:** 71 (White tees) / 75 (Red tees)
**Length:** 5,992yds–6,625yds
**Type:** Links

**Green fees:**
▼ adult per round (Low/Shoulder/High season)
▼ junior per round (March/Shoulder season)

● **JUBILEE COURSE (18 HOLES)**
Originally intended for ladies and beginners when opened in 1897, the Jubilee Course is regarded as the most challenging of all the courses available at St Andrews. Converted to a championship layout in 1988, the course sits in a prime location between the New Course and the sea.

Bookings can be made either online or via the reservations department (+44 (0) 1334 466718) up to two days in advance. Within two days bookings can be made via telephone (+44 (0) 1334 466666) and the starter takes payment on the day before play commences.

**Par:** 72 (White tees) / 74 (Red tees)
**Length:** 5,975yds–6,742yds

**Green fees:**
▼ adult per round (Low/Shoulder/High season)
▼ junior per round (March/Shoulder season)

**Regarded by some as the toughest course at St Andrews, the Jubilee Course has a prime location along the coastline.** *St Andrews Links.*

Solid iron play is required to make a good score on the beautiful **Strathtyrum Course.** *St Andrews Links.*

### ● EDEN COURSE (18 HOLES)

Set slightly back from the coast with some severe bunker tests. The Eden Course was designed by Harry S. Colt and opened in 1914.

Bookings can be made either online or via the reservations department (+44 (0) 1334 466718) up to two days in advance. Within two days bookings can be made via telephone (+44 (0) 1334 466666) and the starter takes payment on the day before play commences.

**Par:** 70 (White tees) / 73 (Red tees)
**Length:** 5,450yds–6,250yds

**Green fees:**
▼ adult per round (Low/Shoulder/High season)
▼ junior per round (March/Shoulder season)

### ● STRATHTYRUM COURSE (18 HOLES)

Opened in 1993 with the aim to compliment the tougher tests on the championship courses. The focus on the Strathtyrum Course is accurate iron play. While there are only fifteen bunkers on the course they're strategically placed to accompany large, sloping, greens.

Bookings can be made either online or via the reservations department (+44 (0) 1334 466718) up to two days in advance. Within two days bookings can be made via telephone (+44 (0) 1334 466666) and the starter takes payment on the day before play commences.

**Par:** 69 (White tees) / 68 (Red tees)
**Length:** 4,705yds–5,620yds

**Green fees:**
▼ adult per round (Low/Shoulder/High season)
▼ junior per round (March/Shoulder season)

### ● BALGOVE COURSE (9 HOLES)

The only 9-hole course within the St Andrews stable and designed to cater for beginners, children and families. A great practice ground for all ages and abilities.

There is no requirement (or facility) to book in advance for the Balgove Course, you can turn up on the day and play.

**Par:** 30
**Length:** 1,520yds

**Green fees:**
▼ adult per round (Low/Shoulder/High season)
▼ junior per round (March/Shoulder season)
(9-hole price guide)

## TRUMP INTERNATIONAL GOLF LINKS

Trump International Golf Links,
Menie Estate,
Balmedie,
Aberdeenshire
AB23 8YE
**www.trumpgolfscotland.com**
**Phone:** +44 (0) 1358 743300
**Email:** bookings@trumpgolfscotland.com

**Essential course details –**
**Par:** 72 (All tees)
**S.S.S:** 77 (Black tees) / 73 (Red tees)
**Slope rating:** 149 (Black tees) / 131 (Red tees)
**Length:** 5,215yds–7,428yds
**Longest hole:** Par-5 18th, 518yds–651yds
**Shortest hole:** Par-3 6th, 128yds–183yds
**Type:** Links

**Handicap Certificate:** Not required

**Green fees:**
(High season)
▼ per round
▼ Scottish & local resident per round
▼ second round (within 7 days)

(Low season)
▼ per round
▼ Scottish & local resident per round
▼ second round (within 7 days)

**Caddies:**
£55 per player per round (+ gratuity).

Caddiemaster – Email:
caddiemaster@trumpgolfscotland.
com / Phone: +44 (0) 1358 74 33 00
(option 4)

### Equipment hire:
Golf clubs, shoes, pull trolleys,
electric trolleys, buggies (limited
number) all available upon request.

### How do I book a round of golf?
The course is unavailable for play
during the winter months, typically
closing between November until the
end of February.

There are three ways to book a
round of golf at Trump International
Golf Links.

*Online:*
Make a request via the online
booking system on the official
website – www.trumpgolfscotland.
com/golf/tee-times

*Phone:*
+44 (0) 1358 743300 (option 1)

*Email:*
bookings@trumpgolfscotland.
com (include all relevant details –
preferred dates/times, group size etc)

**Looking from the tee down towards the green at the par-3 3rd. The closest point on the course to the sea.** *Trump International Golf Links.*

## HISTORY

In a country where golf history stretches back centuries and is rich with tales of how the most hallowed courses came to fruition, Trump International Golf Links still has an interesting story to tell even though it's very much the baby within the group. Despite owning numerous wonderful courses around the world, it was always Donald Trump's vision to build one from scratch and when he saw this particular piece of land and its dramatic location, he knew it was perfect.

The ground was broken and construction of the course commenced in 2010. The design responsibility fell upon revered golf course architect, Dr Martin Hawtree, whose previous work includes the re-design of Royal Birkdale and, more recently, the Old Course, St Andrews.

The course was finally opened, amid much media publicity, on 10 July 2012. Naturally, Donald Trump was present and would hit the first ceremonial tee-shot with members of the European Ryder Cup committee, including Colin Montgomerie, in attendance.

The course resides within the grounds of the private Menie Estate and with further developments planned, the total cost of construction could reach close to a billion dollars.

Whether you agree with Donald Trump's politics or not, his love for golf is without question and it is said, of all the courses he owns around the world, this one is closest to his heart as it is the only one he has witnessed all the way through from design to reality.

## PLAYING THE COURSE

Located within such a secluded, natural, landscape it is quite difficult to imagine another course in Scotland quite like this one. Each hole gives the sense you are the only one playing the course.

Despite its fledgling status, almost all the dunes you see are the work of Mother Nature rather than that of an esteemed golf designer. Hitting your ball into the marram grass may make it almost impossible to find and completely impossible to play.

With the surrounding dunes towering above each hole and the long, wild, rough running tightly alongside the fairways, it is vital that you choose the correct tee in which to play from and with up to six on each hole there are plenty of options depending upon your ability. Be wise rather than brave and you'll enjoy yourself a whole lot more.

Hole 1 is a 491-yard medium-length par-5, reachable in two shots for long hitters. Three cross-bunkers guard the lay-up area for the third shot forcing you to make a choice between attacking or playing safe. Hole 2 offers

The par-5 4th, looking towards the most contoured green on the course, sitting high up within a gap in the dunes. *Trump International Golf Links.*

**The breath-taking view from the tee towards the 14th fairway, surrounded by dunes.**
*Trump International Golf Links.*

**14** **SIGNATURE HOLE: PAR-4 14TH, 255–445YDS.**
The back-9 holes subject you to more stunning, panoramic views, none more so than from the tee box at hole 14. From here you get a grasp of the vastness of the sea beyond the dunes. The hole, the 2nd hardest on the course, is a medium-length par-4 with a very tight fairway that follows the dune valley to the left towards a contoured green. Only the centre of the green will do for your approach shot here.

incredible views of the North Sea from the raised tee box. The Menie Burn bisects this par-4 where only the longest hitters should attempt to hit over it. The green is surrounded by some quite severe hollows should you miss with your approach shot.

Hole 4 is Dr Hawtree's favourite and is also the most difficult on the course. The Blairton Burn runs the along the entire right-hand side of the hole so aim left with your tee-shot and approach towards a heavily contoured green. A par here should be cherished.

The 6th is a real gem of a par-3 with the green partially tucked behind a large dune on the left and Blairton Burn on the right. With a strong south-westerly wind to contend with, the line you take over the dune needs careful thought. Not the longest par-3 but one that can cause some damage to your scorecard with two-thirds of the round still to play.

Holes 8 and 9 are long par-4s with difficult tee-shots along winding fairways. The green at the 8th hole does not have any bunkers to protect it but the surrounding contours should be deemed sufficiently challenging. The long, narrow, green at the 9th hole has three bunkers protecting it, but with only one visible from the fairway, making the club choice for the approach shot an important one.

The last three holes turn you back towards the clubhouse and directly into the prevailing wind. Hole 16 is a 180-yard par-3 with a green protected by seven bunkers, however, the green is quite large and should offset what looks, initially, to be an intimidating tee-shot.

The 18th hole is the longest (651yds from the Black tees) and offers, from the elevated tee, the final exhilarating views of this incredible coastline. However, don't let the majestic view fool you. Of the ninety-four bunkers on the course there are eighteen on this final hole – most lining the right-hand side of the fairway. Two lakes also line the left-hand side. For your final tee-shot let the view be your inspiration, rather than distraction, for a drive straight down the middle.

# 18-hole courses nearby

● **NEWBURGH-ON-YTHAN GOLF CLUB**

Two miles north of Trump International Links, situated on the Ythan Estuary overlooking the Forvie National Nature Reserve. Founded in 1888, this course location is breathtaking.

**Website:** www.newburghgolfclub.co.uk

**Email:** secretary@newburghgolfclub.co.uk
**Telephone:** +44 (0) 1358 789058

**Par:** 72
**Length:** 5,416yds–5,810yds
**Type:** Links

**Fees:**
▼ per round (weekdays & weekends)

**22**

# TRUMP TURNBERRY – AILSA COURSE

Maidens Road,
Turnberry,
Ayrshire,
KA26 9LT
**www.turnberry.co.uk**
Phone: +44 (0) 1655 331000
Email: teetimes@trumpturnberry.com

**Essential course details –**
**Par:** 71 (Black tees) / 74 (Red tees)
**S.S.S:** 77 (Black tees) / 72 (Red tees)
**Slope rating:** 139 (Black tees) / 127 (Red tees)
**Length:** 5,406yds–7,489yds
**Longest hole:** Par-5 7th, 420yds–575yds
**Shortest hole:** Par-3 6th, 103yds–171yds
**Type:** Links

**Handicap Certificate:** Not required

**Green fees:**
**(High season)**
▼ hotel guests per round
▼ visitors per round

**(Shoulder season)**
▼ hotel guests per round
▼ visitors per round

**(Low season)**
▼ hotel guests per round
▼ visitors per round

**Caddies:**
£50 per person per round (+ gratuity)

**Equipment hire:**
£50 – clubs

**How do I book a round of golf?**
There are three ways to book a round
for the Ailsa Course at Turnberry:

*Online:*
www.booktrumpgolf.com (via main
website)

*Phone:*
+44 1655 334032 or +44 1655 334060

*Email:*
teetimes@trumpturnberry.com
(include all relevant details –
preferred dates/times, group size etc)

## HISTORY

Robert The Bruce, the man who
would emerge triumphant from the
War of Scottish Independence and
reclaim Scotland's right to be an
independent country, usually tops
most polls of revered Scottish figures
from history.

Turnberry Castle is recognised,
albeit disputed, to be Bruce's
birthplace as it was the family seat
of his mother, Marjorie of Carrick – a
formidable woman. Upon hearing
from a young man sent to inform
her of her husband's death during
a crusade, Marjorie fell so in love
with him she had him imprisoned in

the castle until he agreed to marry her. This young man was Robert De Brus – Robert The Bruce's father.

Having fallen into enemy hands on two occasions previously, the castle would be destroyed, upon orders given by Bruce himself, in 1310 during the war of independence in order to remove any hope the English had of occupying it ever again. No attempt was made to rebuild it.

The ruins of the castle are now surrounded on three sides by the Ayrshire coastline, on the land once occupied by the castle there now sits a lighthouse with a golf course directly in front of it – the Ailsa Course.

The Marquess of Ailsa commissioned local course designer and former Open Champion, Willie Fernie to design an 18-hole course on the site in 1900. Golf was first played on the brand new course in 1901 and the following year (1902) saw the creation of the Turnberry Golf Club. Requisitioned during both world wars as an airbase, the course came close to full closure. Reopened in 1951, the course would have to wait a further twenty-six years to host its first Open Championship, but it was worth the wait.

The legendary tussle between Nicklaus and Watson in the final round of the 1977 tournament is now part of The Open folklore and one of the greatest finales to a championship in modern memory. To commemorate this classic event the 18th hole was renamed 'Duel in the Sun'.

## PLAYING THE COURSE

The Ailsa course is, arguably, the most visually stunning place to play golf anywhere in the world. However, don't let its beauty lull you into a false sense of security – this is a tough course, particularly when the wind is blowing in from the Firth of Clyde.

Before you reach the coast holes, you have three very testing par-4 holes to contend with. The 1st hole has a slight dogleg to the right with an intimidating tee-shot towards a large gorse trap. Bunkers await at the front of the green for anything short. The 2nd hole translates as 'Make Sure', aptly its important to make sure you avoid the numerous fairway bunkers. The long par-4 3rd hole is one of the most testing on the course – an accurate drive is crucial. Anything right from the tee will be in very long rough.

The next eight holes will test your concentration to the maximum as they reside along one the most beautiful stretches of coastline Scotland has to offer.

The 4th hole is the first of five par-3s and the first real test with green and tee-box separated by a large patch of, purpose built, sandy wasteland. At a tricky length of around 180yds to clear, anything short could be out of bounds.

**The 1st hole, named after Ailsa Craig, which is visible from almost every hole on the course.**
*Steve Carr Golf.*

The green is right next to the beach so accuracy from the tee is crucial.

The 5th is the first par-5 and is definitely reachable in two shots for any long hitter, the 6th is a short par-3. Holes 7 and 8 are generally regarded as being among the hardest on the course. The 8th in particular is a tough, long par-4 with two fairway bunkers acting like magnets at around 300yds as the ground slopes down towards them.

The final six holes all head back inland towards the clubhouse and include two of the most difficult holes on the course – 16th and 17th. The 16th is named after the burn running across the front of the green. Aim right with your tee-shot to give the best angle into the green and over the burn with your approach. The literal translation of the name for the 17th ('Lang Whang') means 'Long Whack' and you need to give your ball two big whacks to make the green here. If you avoid the fairway bunker your approach shot needs to carry a steep ridge to make it up to the green.

The par-4 18th hole looks completely straight down towards the hotel. The tee-box offers the last glimpse of the ocean with Ailsa Craig directly behind you. A wonderful way to finish a truly beautiful course.

The 9th tee with Turnberry Lighthouse and the ruins of Turnberry Castle in the distance. Quite possibly the most breathtaking view from a tee box anywhere in the world. *Steve Carr Golf.*

**9**
**10**
**11**

**SIGNATURE HOLE(S): PAR-3 9TH 143-248YDS /PAR-5 10TH 371-565YDS / PAR-3 11TH 115-215YDS.**

Augusta has 'Amen Corner', Turnberry has 'Lighthouse Edge'. A major re-design in 2015 saw changes to large parts of the course, but it is here that these changes have had the most dramatic effect. Previously it was felt that the standard of the holes did not match the majesty of the surroundings but now, finally, the most famous section of this course has three holes it can be proud of.

The **9th**, formerly a fairly short par-4, is now a par-3. What hasn't changed is the tee-shot over the rocks towards the lighthouse. This could be the most visually stunning hole you ever drop a shot(s) on, so don't be too hard on yourself. Be sure to respect the carry distance, commit to a line you're confident you can make and stick to it.

The **10th**, formerly a par-4, is now regarded as potentially becoming one of the most challenging par-5s on the championship circuit. A dogleg left from the tee and a green sat on the rocks where the old 11th tee used to reside – going long with your approach isn't advisable.

The **11th** is still a par-3 but much longer. Previously seen as a birdie opportunity by the pros during Open week, the hole is now a different animal. Like the 9th, it's another big gulp before a tee-shot over the rocks to a green that sits right beside the beach.

**View from behind the 11th green. Anything short or long could end up on the rocks.** *Getty Images.*

# Other courses on site

In addition to the Ailsa Course, Trump Turnberry also has the following courses available for visitors to play:

## ● KING ROBERT THE BRUCE (18 HOLES)

Opened in June 2017 on the site of the former Kintyre course, the King Robert the Bruce course offers very fine support to its more illustrious championship sibling. Many of the holes have been totally transformed and all the bunkers overhauled to provide a very tough links test in its own right.

**Par:** 72 (Black tees) / 74 (White tees)
**Length:** 5,767yds–7,203yds

### Green fees:

▼ hotel guests per round (high season)
▼ hotel guests per round (low/shoulder season)
▼ visitors per round (high season)
▼ visitors per round (low/shoulder season)
▼ combination ticket* (hotel guests & visitors)

*The combination ticket includes a round on both King Robert the Bruce and Ailsa. Visitors must play both courses on the same day, hotel guests have the option to play on separate days.

## ● ARRAN (9 HOLES)

Solid 9-hole course with a good combination of four par-4s and five par-3s.

**Par:** 31
**Length:** 3,730yds–3,992yds

### Green fees:

▼ hotel guests per round (high season)
▼ hotel guests per round (low season)
▼ hotel guests per round (shoulder season)
▼ visitors per round (high season)
▼ visitors per round (low/shoulder season)
(9-hole price guide)

# WESTERN GAILES GOLF CLUB

Western Gailes Golf Club,
Gailes,
Irvine,
Ayrshire,
KA11 5AE
**www.westerngailes.com**
**Phone:** +44 (0) 1294 311649
**Email:** enquiries@westerngailes.com

**Essential course details –**

**Par:** 71

**S.S.S:** 74 (White tees) / 68 (Green tees)

**Slope rating:** 137 (White tees) / 126 (Green tees)

**Length:** 5,441yds–6,640yds

**Longest hole:** Par-5 14th, 425yds–562yds

**Shortest hole:** Par-3 13th, 125yds–141yds

**Type:** Links

**Handicap Certificate:** Not required

**Green fees:**
▼ per round
▼ two rounds (Weekdays – includes lunch & course guide)

**Caddies:**
£45 per person per round (+ gratuity). Book in advance.

**Equipment hire:**
£5 – pull trolleys
£35 – golf clubs
£40 – buggy (six available)

## How do I book a round of golf?

Western Gailes Golf Club is a private members club; however, visitor bookings are available for the following times during the week –

| | |
|---|---|
| Monday | 9.00 am–12.00 noon & 2.00 pm–4.30 pm |
| Tuesday | 2.00 pm–3.00 pm |
| Wednesday | 9.00 am–12.00 noon & 2.00 pm–4.30 pm |
| Thursday | 2.00 pm–3.00 pm |
| Friday | 9.00 am–12.00 noon & 2.00 pm–4.30 pm |
| Saturday | 3.30 pm–4.30 pm |
| Sunday | 2.30 pm–4.00 pm |

There are three ways to book a round of golf at Western Gailes Golf Club:

*Online:*
www.westerngailesgolfclub.com/bookings

*Phone:*
+44 (0) 1294 311649

*Email:*
enquiries@westerngailes.com
(include all relevant details – preferred dates/times, group size etc)

## HISTORY

Towards the end of the nineteenth century, in the midst of the industrial revolution, a group of Glasgow merchants sought solace away from the hustle and bustle of the city. They had a vision for a golf course along the Ayrshire coast that would be free from winter frost and allow play all year round. Rather than become members of some of the more famous clubs already in existence nearby, they chose to create their own.

Founded in 1897, the club leased land from the Duke of Portland and initially laid down a 9-hole course with a further nine added quite rapidly the following year. The 130-acre site lies between the sea and the railway line, which allowed easy access to and from Glasgow for its members. Initially a two-storey temporary clubhouse was erected before a permanent structure was opened, at a cost of £4,000, in 1909.

While the course has never hosted the Open Championship, it has served as the final qualifying site for the various Ayrshire-area Opens at Troon and Turnberry and has also hosted several famous matches. Harry Vardon, member of the Great Triumvirate, won the first significant championship to be held at the course in 1903 and in the succeeding decades, Western Gailes has hosted a succession of top Scottish amateur and pro events from the juniors, seniors and Scottish Open.

## PLAYING THE COURSE

The Western Gailes course, as mentioned in the history section, is situated between the sea and a railway line. Both of which are very much in play for any wayward golf shot. As the name suggests, gales of wind and rain have always played a major factor in the course design and conditions. Wind is almost a constant factor coming off the nearby Firth, adding distance to the shortest of holes and making the par-4s and 5s much more difficult to reach in regulation.

**Railway line in the distance and a burn running in front of the green. The par-4 8th at Western Gailes represents all that is great about links golf.** *Mark Alexander Golf Photography.*

View from the back of the par-3 7th, one of the most memorable par-3s Scotland has to offer. *Mark Alexander Golf Photography.*

(7) **SIGNATURE HOLE: PAR-3 7TH, 141–171YDS, 'SEA'.**
Without doubt the most picturesque, most photographed and most talked about hole on the course. When you play Western Gailes for the first time, this is probably the one hole that you'll still remember many years later. One of the most terrific links par-3s Scotland has to offer. The hole is flanked either side by large dunes and is almost all carry up to the green. Your tee-shot must be straight and accurate towards a green sloping away from the sea and surrounded by six bunkers. Anything short won't carry, left and long could well be unplayable.

The first five holes are all par-4s of varying difficulty and length. The 1st is a gentle start. Aim the drive towards the right of the fairway – using the road bridge as your line. Any approach shot which is short runs the risk of the ball running back into a deep hollow at the front. Go too far left and the ball will run off the green. The same guidance applies off the tee at the 2nd with anything left potentially becoming a card wrecker before the round even gets going so aim for the railway line on the right.

For the next nine holes – 5th through to 13th – the sea is a constant

**The 18th green with stunning views looking out over the Firth of Clyde.** *Mark Alexander Golf Photography.*

companion on your right-hand side. Hole 5 is the toughest on the course – a long par-4 with a very narrow fairway into the green requiring two well-struck shots to get there. Hole 6 is the first par-5. Aim for the clubhouse with your drive. A pole marks the back right of the green and will assist with your approach shot.

Another stretch of five par-4s follows. Do not go right at hole 10, if anything it may be best to give up some yards as a burn sits right before the green hence a short iron would be the wiser approach. The 11th plays second hardest hole with a fairway angled left to right presenting a tough tee-shot. You should be able to see a railway signal box in the distance – aim for that and you will be fine.

Reaching the 13th hole, a tricky par-3 surrounded by small pot bunkers that you don't want to be in, you may notice the wind slightly changing direction. By the 14th the wind should be right behind you but this still plays like the longest hole and requires a tee-shot left of centre. The approach shot is tough into a long narrow green.

Club members will tell you, in their opinion, the par-4 17th is the most difficult hole on the course. The railway runs all the way down the right-hand side and presents a real challenge off the tee. However, this often results in drives heading into the fairway bunker 228yds on the left. Your ideal line is the left edge of the clubhouse. There is just one bunker front-right of the green that catches far more balls than it should so the approach can be long to avoid this.

The round concludes with a 377-yard par-4. The starters hut offers you the line in for your tee-shot, ensuring you avoid the four fairway bunkers spread along the right. The bunker front-left is quite short of the green, which always plays longer than it looks. The green has some subtle slopes making your final putt quite tricky.

# 18-hole courses nearby

● **GAILES LINKS GOLF COURSE**
Opened in 1892 by Glasgow Golf Club (9th oldest Golf Club in the world) and designed by revered golf architect, Willie Park Jnr. Considered a world class links course and typically used for final qualifying in Scotland when The Open is held at either Troon or Turnberry.

This course is definitely a tough cookie. Famous for its gorse-lined fairways, you need a steady hand here to ensure your driving is straight down the middle. The railway line lurks near to the course presenting lots of 'out of bounds' opportunities for any wayward shots.

A classic links course with tight fairways, well positioned bunkers and challenging greens.

**Website:** www.gaileslinks.co.uk
**Email:** admin@gaileslinks.co.uk
**Telephone:** +44 (0) 1419 422011 (Option 1)

**Par:** 71
**Length:** 5,553yds–6,903yds
**Type:** Links

**Fees:**
▼ per round (after 1.30 pm at weekends)

# COURSES OF SPECIAL SIGNIFICANCE

## SHISKINE GOLF CLUB – 12-HOLE COURSE

Shiskine Golf & Tennis Club,
Shore Road,
Blackwaterfoot,
Isle of Arran,
KA27 8HA
**www.shiskinegolf.com**
**Phone:** +44 (0) 1770 860226
**Email:** info@shiskinegolf.com

**Essential course details –**
**Par:** 42 (Yellow tees)
**S.S.S:** 41 (Yellow tees)
(an 18-hole to 12-hole handicap conversion chart is available on the Club website)
**Length:** 2,770yds
**Longest hole:** Par-5 9th, 479yds
**Shortest hole:** Par-3 12th, 118yds
**Type:** Links

**Handicap Certificate:** Not required

**Green fees:**
▼ per round (weekdays & weekends)
▼ day tickets* (weekdays & weekends)
*not available during July and August

**Caddies:** Not available

**Equipment hire:**
Buggies, pull trolleys and clubs are available upon request and can be booked in advance from the Pro shop; +44 (0) 1770 860226.

**How do I book a round of golf?**
Shiskine Golf & Tennis Club is a private members club; however, visitors are welcome to play any day during the week.

There are two ways to book a round of golf at Shiskine Golf Club:

**Phone:**
+44 (0) 1770 860226

**Online:**
www.shiskinegolf.com (via Home page)

## HISTORY

The Club and course were originally opened in 1896. Willie Fernie was the main architect who designed the initial 9-hole layout. The 5th and 9th holes are the only survivors from the original concept.

The course would be extended to 18 holes following the acquirement of

The 5th green at Shiskine with a sailing ship on Kilbrannan Sound in the distance. *Hamish Bannatyne.*

sufficient land in September 1912. Six of the holes were located on Drumadoon Hill, however, during the First World War they reverted to their natural state and were deemed unplayable.

Willie Park was responsible for the design of the existing 12-hole layout between 1925–28. Initially the first six holes would be played twice in order to complete an 18-hole round. Nowadays most competitions are played over 12 holes but when 18 holes are required, holes 1, 2, 9, 11 and 12 are replayed along with an artificial 15th using a new tee from the 3rd to the 4th green.

## PLAYING THE COURSE

The course at Shiskine has achieved cult status for many who have been lucky enough to play its unique 12-hole layout. It isn't just the number of holes that make the course so sought after by golfing enthusiasts around the globe, it's also the majestic location looking out towards the Kintyre peninsula.

This is a course that requires true focus, as you will find yourself having to make many blind shots, both from the tee and on the approach, as you make your way around the tough terrain. There are lots of stop/go signals and markers to assist you as you go. A round of golf here should take no more than

**A sloping green awaits at the signature, par-3, 3rd hole.**
*Hamish Bannatyne.*

**3** **SIGNATURE HOLE: PAR-3 3RD, 121YDS, 'CROWS NEST'.**
Only a short par-3 but this is the hole everyone talks about the most after their round. Take more club than you need and avoid going left as anything here will be lost. There's plenty of room along the right-hand side but you may be left with a difficult downhill putt for your par.

a couple of hours, so it's well worth considering making a day of it and going round more than once.

The 1st is a tough opening hole with the beach on the left representing out of bounds, and a blind approach shot needs to be short rather than long. Hole 2 has out of bounds along the right with another blind approach shot where you need to avoid the burn in front of the green.

Two more par-3s follow at holes 4 and 5. The 4th is another memorable tee-shot from an elevated position. The 5th is a long one at 211yds and can play into a cross-wind. Anything long will leave a difficult chip to the green to save your score.

Holes 6,7 and 8 are all quite straightforward, offering excellent opportunities to improve your scorecard before you reach the par-5 9th. Here your tee-shot offers you lots of room to cover up any errors. Best to lay up before the burn on the fairway for the best line into the green. The tee box from the 10th will have you reaching for your camera, offering an incredible 360-degree panorama. As with previous par-3s, it's best to be short rather than long at this hole.

You finish your round with two more par-3s. The 12th is the shortest hole on the course at 118yds. The green has two bunkers on the left and one short right waiting to catch any stray tee-shots.

**Glorious view from the tee at the 7th hole looking out towards Kintyre.** *Hamish Bannatyne.*

## MUSSELBURGH LINKS – THE OLD GOLF COURSE

Musselburgh Links, The Old Golf Course,
Stables Pavilion,
Balcarres Road,
Musselburgh,
EH21 7SR
**www.musselburgholdlinks.co.uk**
**Phone:** 0131 653 5122
**Email:** oldlinks@enjoyleisure.com

**Essential course details –**
**Par:** 34 (White tees) / 36 (Red tees)
**Length:** 2,734yds–2,954yds
**Longest hole:** par-5 7th, 472yds–479yds
**Shortest hole:** par-3 5th, 177yds–183yds
**Type:** Links

**Handicap Certificate:** Not required

**Green fees:**
Monday–Friday
▼ per adult (9 holes)
▼ seniors (over 60s)
▼ under 18s & young Scot Card
   Holder (Under 26)
Saturday-Sunday
▼ per adult (9 holes)
▼ seniors (over 60s)
▼ under 18s & young Scot Card
   Holder (Under 26)

**Caddies & equipment hire:**
£23 – modern clubs (per round)
£39 – hickory clubs (per round)
£4.30 – push trolley

### How do I book a round of golf?

Musselburgh Links is open to the public all year round, with the exception of Christmas Day and New Years Day.

When there is a race fixture at Musselburgh Racecourse, only a limited number of tee times are available. Race fixture dates can be found on the Musselburgh Racecourse website – www.musselburgh-racecourse.co.uk.

There are two ways to book a round of golf for The Old Golf Course:

*Phone:*
+44 (0) 131 653 5122

*Email:*
oldlinks@enjoyleisure.com (include all relevant details – preferred dates/times, group size etc)

### HISTORY

A site that can lay claim to being the oldest playable golf course in the world, how's that for history? Legend has it that Mary Stuart, Queen of Scots, (1542–1587), played golf at Musselburgh in 1567. The first clear evidence of golf played at the course was by prominent Edinburgh Lawyer, Sir John Foulis of Ravelston, in 1672. A studious recorder of golf events, Foulis lost a match with his friends Gosford and Lyon as his account book records:

1672

Mar 2 Lost at Golfe at Musselboorgh with Gosford, Lyon etc .. .. £3 5s 0d

(Source: www.scottishgolfhistory.org)

Musselburgh was one of the original Open Championship venues along with Prestwick and St Andrews, hosting the event on six occasions between 1874 and 1889. Some of Musselburgh's former residents read as a veritable who's who from golf's rich history – Fiery John Carey, The Dunn twins, Willie Campbell and John Gourlay to name a few. St Andrews has the Old Course but Musselburgh Links has the oldest course.

## BALCARRES ROAD

Musselburgh Links may not be at the centre of the golfing universe these days but when you visit the course, you can still see evidence of The Old Golf Course's vibrant history.

At one stage, during the nineteenth century when The Old Golf Course regularly shared hosting of The Open Championship, four of the most prominent golf societies played at Musselburgh Links during the same period and their clubhouses can still be seen today. As you approach the visitor's pavilion, along Balcarres Road (formerly known as Links Place), the first old clubhouse you'll see is now known as Wiremill Social Club. It was built in 1886 by Brunstfield Links Golfing Society and was used by its members for twelve years.

**Approach towards the long par-3 1st green with the racecourse track and stand behind.**
*Musselburgh Links, The Old Golf Course.*

**Bruntsfield Links old Clubhouse now the Wiremill Social Club.** *www.scottishgolfhistory.org*

About 100yds further down the road you come to a nursery (Links Nursery). Over 150 years ago members of The Honourable Company of Edinburgh Golfers used this building before they moved to Muirfield in 1891. Next door to the nursery is the former Clubhouse of The Royal Musselburgh Golf Club, constructed in 1873 and used by members until 1908 at which time they moved next door into the old HCEG Clubhouse. The Club eventually departed in 1925

**HCEG old Clubhouse, 8 Balcarres Road.**
*www.scottishgolfhistory.org*

**Royal Burgess Golf Society old Clubhouse, 10 Balcarres Road.** *www.scottishgolfhistory.org*

and moved into their current home down the road at Prestongrange House.

The next building on from Royal Musselburgh's former home, you will see the previous residence of the oldest Golf Club in the world – The Royal Burgess Golfing Society. Built in 1875, Royal Burgess used the building for twenty years before moving to Barnton. The building is now used by the Musselburgh Old Course Golf Club who still play their golf on the Old Links.

At the front of this building you will see a plaque in honour of the four Musselburgh-based players who won The Open during the six years when The Old Golf Course hosted the competition.

## PLAYING THE COURSE

Musselburgh Links draws players to its course not only because of its history but also for its exclusive position within the perimeter of a horseracing track. The golf came first, the race track followed in 1816 due to there being no other suitable land available. Sadly there are no longer any ocean views to enjoy while you play due to a major land fill renovation undertaken following the closure of Cockenzie Power Station.

Despite all this, it is still a true links layout where the test lies in the undulations of the fairways, the placing of bunkers, the shape of the greens and, of course, winds. Musselburgh has all of these features.

**View from the back of the 6th green with Arthur's Seat in the background.**
*Musselburgh Links, The Old Golf Course.*

The 1st hole, an incredibly daunting start (240-yard, par-3), requires an accurate tee-shot to a well-defended green with right to left cross-winds. Hole 2 is the first of three par-4s in a row (and five overall). Look out for two bunkers well placed around three quarters of the way down the fairway. Hole 3 requires a straight drive with heavy gorse protecting the left side of the fairway and the racetrack on the right.

The 4th hole – Mrs Forman's – used to be a popular resting point for drinks. You don't get one, though, until you've navigated through a semi-blind tee-shot and tricky approach onto an undulating green with few opportunities for a straight putt. The par-3 5th is a testing hole with the green well protected by bunkers.

The 6th offers stunning views of Arthur's Seat. The line here is down the left giving you a straight shot onto the green.

The 7th is the only par-5 and, at 479yds, offers a good chance for birdie with a very large green to aim for. Hole 8 is a long, uphill par-3 with tee-shots often going into the prevailing wind – club choice is key here. Finally the 9th brings you in with a heavily bunkered par-4 and long rough protecting the side of the fairway. A tough finishing hole to a truly unique experience.

# Other courses of historical significance nearby

## ● THE ROYAL BURGESS GOLFING SOCIETY OF EDINBURGH

At the other side of Edinburgh from the world's oldest playable golf course you will find the present home of reputedly the world's oldest Golf Club, founded in 1735. Visitors are welcome to play the course at Barnton, originally designed by Willie Park Jr in 1895 and modified by James Braid in the 1920s, seven days a week.

**Website:** www.royalburgess.co.uk
**Email:** enquiries@royalburgess.co.uk
**Telephone:** +44 (0) 131 339 2075

**Par:** 71 (Red tees) / 73 (Yellow tees)
**Length:** 5,704yds–6,531yds
**Type:** Parkland

**Fees:**
▼ per round
(18-hole price guide)

## ● THE BRUNTSFIELD LINKS GOLFING SOCIETY

Next door to the oldest Golf Club in the world you'll find the present home of the fourth oldest. Established in 1761, like Royal Burgess, the members of Bruntsfield Links moved to their current residence after Musselburgh Links became overcrowded. Visitors are welcome to play the course seven days a week.

**Website:** www.bruntsfieldlinks.co.uk
**Email:** info@bruntsfieldlinks.co.uk
**Telephone:** +44 (0) 131 336 1479

**Par:** 70 (White tees) / 68 (Blue tees)
**Length:** 5,427yds–6,437yds
**Type:** Parkland

**Fees:**
▼ per round
(18-hole price guide)

# 9-HOLE COURSES

## ANSTRUTHER GOLF CLUB

Marsfield House,
Shore Road,
Anstruther,
KY10 3DZ
www.anstruthergolf.co.uk
Phone: +44 (0) 1333 310956
Email: clubhouse@anstruthergolf.
co.uk

**Essential course details –**
**Par:** 31 (White tees) / 33 (Red tees)
**Length:** 2,064yds–2,249yds
**Longest hole:** Par-4 8th, 410yds
**Shortest hole:** Par-3 2nd, 142yds
**Type:** Links

**Handicap Certificate:** Not required

**Green fees:**

**December, January, February –**
▼ per adult per round (both 18 or 9 holes)
▼ juniors (under 16)

**March–November**
▼ per adult per round (9 holes)
▼ per adult per round (18 holes)
▼ juniors (for 9 or 18 holes)

**Equipment hire:**
Available upon request

**How do I book a round of golf?**
Bookings are not normally required, but may be advisable in July and August and also for large groups (10+).

For bookings during this period contact the club via email bookings@anstruthergolf.co.uk (include all relevant details – preferred dates/times, group size etc.) or phone +44 (0) 1333 310956.

## HISTORY

Anstruther Golf Club was founded in 1890 and has seen many changes over the years. Old Tom Morris was involved in the original layout, which comprised of 7 holes with trenches through the middle of the course and poles scattered over the greens to stop gliders landing during the war. In more peaceful times the course was extended to 9 holes and is open all year round.

The course is located 9 miles south of St Andrews and offers spectacular views over Anstruther

Sunrise at Anstruther Golf Club. The green at the par-3 2nd, called 'Monument', sits proudly in the shadow of the War Memorial with the Isle of May in the distance. *Audrey Peddie.*

Harbour out to the Isle of May, Bass Rock and southwest towards Edinburgh. Anstruther has its own version of Augusta's 'Amen Corner' comprising a trio of challenging par-3s beginning with the signature 5th hole (The Rockies), previously voted the toughest par-3 in the UK.

## PLAYING THE COURSE

The 1st hole is an uphill par-4 with a blind approach-shot needing to navigate past a bunker to the right of the green. The 2nd is the first par-3 with a well-protected green, three bunkers front and right and thick rough at the rear. Hole 3 is a slight dogleg playing into the wind. The drive needs to be left of centre to open up the green, protected by five bunkers mainly on the right.

**5** SIGNATURE HOLE: **PAR-3 5TH, 245YDS, THE ROCKIES.**
After a straightforward par-4 4th you move on to the toughest hole on the course. From the elevated tee you must hit the ball onto the small fairway, which is guarded on the right by thick gorse and a rough covered bank. The left side is covered by the Firth of Forth which is, obviously, out of bounds. An experienced golfer can go for the green in one but there's no shame in playing this hole as a par-4.

**The old Clubhouse still resides next to the fairway on the 3rd hole at Anstruther.** *Anstruther Golf Club.*

Hole 6 has a wide but narrow green with a bank of gorse protecting the back. The 7th is a smaller, par-3, version of the 1st with a 30ft hill and rough to the left. It's advised to take one more club than you think for this hole.

Hole 8 is an excellent par-4. Use the monument as the line off the tee. Five fairway bunkers await any wayward shots. The 9th hole plays down hill towards the first tee and is generally down wind. This hole is not as simple as it seems with its length and wall behind the green its main defences.

**Aerial view of the course and surrounding town at Anstruther.** *Anstruther Golf Club*

# BRIDGE OF ALLAN GOLF CLUB

Bridge of Allan Golf Club,
Sunnylaw,
Bridge of Allan,
FK9 4LY
**www.bofagc.com**
**Phone:** +44 (0) 1786 832332
**Email:** marketing@bofagc.com

**Essential course details –**
**Par:** 33 (White & Red tees)
**Length:** 2,267yds–2,560yds
**Longest hole:** Par-4 8th, 315yds–390yds
**Shortest hole:** Par-3 9th, 158yds–167yds
**Type:** Inland

**Handicap Certificate:** Not required

**Green fees:**
**April to October**
▼ adult 9 holes
▼ adult 18 holes
▼ adult day ticket
▼ under 18s 9 or 18 holes
▼ under 18s day ticket

**November to March**
▼ adult 9 holes
▼ adult 18 holes
▼ under 18s

**Caddies & equipment hire:**
The club has a limited number of golf clubs available. If you need

to book golf clubs or trolleys you should enter these requirements in the booking form or alternatively you can contact the club directly: +44 (0) 01786 832332.

## How do I book a round of golf?
There are three ways to book a round of golf at Bridge Of Alan Golf Club:

*Online:* www.bofagc.com/teetimes

*Phone:* +44 (0) 01786 832332

*Email:* marketing@bofagc.com (include all relevant details – preferred dates/times, group size etc)

## HISTORY
Designed by Old Tom Morris, Bridge of Allan is a 9-hole golf course dating back to 1895. It's a layout designed for vista lovers, offering picturesque views of the surrounding countryside, including Stirling Castle.

The course has evolved over the years, being now longer than the original layout but many holes are unchanged and original features such as stone dykes across some fairways have been retained.

## PLAYING THE COURSE
In his book *The Golf Courses of Old Tom Morris*, renowned golf historian

Robert Kroeger describes the Bridge of Allan course as the best preserved of any Morris design in that the layout and length of holes and greens are exactly the same as they were in 1895. The course sits on a hill above the spa town where it takes its name and is a stern test for golfers of all ability.

Holes 2, 3 and 4 are all fairly short par-4s where out of bounds awaits any tee-shots too far left. The 4th is another green that is guarded by a wall at the front – a favourite hazard used often by Old Tom. Hole 5 is a long par-3 with a downward tee-shot towards a green placed on a severely sloping hillside. Anything off the green will leave a difficult shot to save par.

Another trio of par-4s follow at holes 6,7 and 8. The 6th has not one but two blind shots to face before getting to the elevated green. The 7th tempts you to drive for the green over a large old oak tree. However, trouble awaits anything hit too far left here. Hole 8 is all uphill and again your hitting

**Terrific aerial view of the 2nd, 3rd, 4th and 6th holes at Bridge of Allan.** *Bridge of Allan Golf Club.*

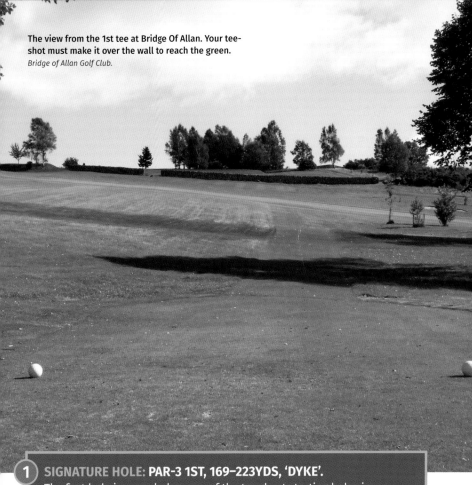

The view from the 1st tee at Bridge Of Allan. Your tee-shot must make it over the wall to reach the green.
*Bridge of Allan Golf Club.*

**1** **SIGNATURE HOLE: PAR-3 1ST, 169–223YDS, 'DYKE'.**
The first hole is regarded as one of the toughest starting holes in Scotland – 223yds from the white and yellow tees – and is listed as one of Old Tom Morris' favourite holes. Originally a par-4, an uphill tee-shot is made all the harder by a 5ft stone wall that protects the green.

blind both off the tee and with your approach.

The 9th, 167-yard par-3, is a great finish with a downhill tee-shot to a sloping green. Anything too firm could go through to heavy rough. Make sure this one is right at the centre.

## CARRBRIDGE GOLF CLUB

Carrbridge Golf Club,
Inverness Rd,
Carrbridge,
PH23 3AU
**www.carrbridgegolf.co.uk**
Phone: +44 (0) 1479 841623
Email: secretary@carrbridgegolf.co.uk

**9th green and Clubhouse basking in glorious sunshine at Carrbridge.** *Carrbridge Golf Club.*

**Essential course details –**
**Par:** 36 (White & Red tees)
**Length:** 2,401yds–2,720yds
**Longest hole:** Par-5 1st, 473yds–480yds
**Shortest hole:** Par-3 8th, 165yds–174yds
**Type:** Inland

**Green fees:**
▼ adult per round (9 holes)
▼ adult day ticket
▼ junior per round (9 holes)
▼ junior day ticket

**Honesty Box:**
▼ May to September after 6 pm
▼ October to March

**Caddies & equipment hire:**
£10 – clubs per round
£2 – push trolley
£10 / £18 – buggies 9 holes / 18 holes
(two available)

**How do I book a round of golf?**
The course is open all year round, weather permitting, and if the clubhouse is closed then an honesty box policy is in operation.

It is recommended to book a tee-time in advance via the club website – www.carrbridgegolf.co.uk/contact-us/

Alternatively, you can contact the club directly via phone or email:

*Phone:* +44 (0) 01479 841623

*Email:* secretary@carrbridgegolf.co.uk

## HISTORY

Carrbridge Golf Club was formed in 1980 but there has been a golf course on the site for many years. The course has been moulded around the natural contours of the land and so offers few man-made hazards. Burns abound and there is water somewhere on every hole. The course rises to about 1,000ft offering excellent views of the Cairngorm Mountains.

## PLAYING THE COURSE

With the exception of the 1st (par-5) and the 8th (par-3) all the holes are par-4s.

**Stunning scenery behind the 2nd green.** *Carrbridge Golf Club.*

Hole 1 requires a drive over the marker towards the paddock. The sensible play is to go for the green in three with careful mid-short iron play towards a green that slopes left to right. You must get your tee-shot right on this hole. For the 2nd hole tee-shot use the clubhouse as your line, a good drive will leave a mid-iron to the green. A road lies before the green so best to go long than risk anything short hitting tarmac. Better to aim right of the green rather than left. Hole 3 needs nothing to be hooked or sliced from the tee. Two bunkers protect the green with out of bounds behind.

The 4th hole requires another straight drive over the hill with out of bounds on your right. The approach shot can be long rather than short as this may result in your ball rolling back towards you. Hole 5 is a driveable par-4 but danger lurks on the left and right. Two bunkers protect a difficult sloping green so don't be too down if you 3-putt here. The 6th green slopes right to left and away from you, therefore, be mindful of your approach shot.

The 8th is the only par-3 with anything left skirting with out of bounds and anything right flirting with greenside bunkers. The 9th is a relatively straightforward par-4 to finish with a wide fairway offering plenty of scope with your drive. If you're playing 18 holes, the second time around this hole plays as a par-3.

**7** **SIGNATURE HOLE: PAR-4 7TH, 218–262YDS, 'EYRIE'.**
Hole 7 offers incredible views of the Cairngorms. The key here is the approach shot, which must land on the elevated green. If you're too short your ball will stick on the bank, if you're long your ball will roll to the bottom of a very steep bank behind the green.

## COMRIE GOLF CLUB

Comrie Golf Club,
Laggan Braes,
Comrie,
Perthshire,
**www.comriegolf.co.uk**
Phone: +44 (0) 1764 670055
Email: info@comriegolf.co.uk

### Essential course details –

**Par:** 35 (White tees) / 37 (Red tees)
**Length:** 2,624yds–3,008yds
**Longest hole:** Par-5 6th, 439yds–493yds
**Shortest hole:** Par-3 5th, 132yds–173yds
**Type:** Mix of Parkland, Heathland and
Hillside

**Handicap Certificate:** Not required

**Green fees:**
▼ adult, 9 holes
▼ adult, 18 holes
▼ under-18, 9 holes
▼ under-18, 18 holes

**Caddies & equipment hire:**
£10 – buggy (9 holes) / £20 (18 holes)
£3 – trolley
No charge for club hire

### How do I book a round of golf?

There are two ways to book a round
of golf at Comrie Golf Club:

*Phone:* +44 (0) 01764 670055

*Email:* info@comriegolf.co.uk (include
all relevant details – preferred dates/
times, group size etc)

### HISTORY

Established in 1891, Comrie is
regarded as one of the most scenic
9-hole courses in the UK with
stunning views over Comrie, Glen
Artney and the hills of western
Perthshire. Part of the Association of
James Braid Courses, the legendary
golf architect suggested changes to
the course during the 1920s, which
were subsequently adopted. The
vistas from the course are worth the
green fee alone.

Every hole has its own distinctive
character, as may be expected of a
course in whose design Braid had a
hand, and no two holes are remotely
the same.

A capercaillie (a member of the
grouse family) took up residency
on the course and surrounding
woodland during the 1980s. This
increasingly rare bird left such an
impression it was adopted as the
Club's emblem, created by former
member and artist, Ian R. Oates.

### PLAYING THE COURSE

The 1st hole is a par-4 with a slight
dogleg right up to a green sloping

4th fairway looking towards the Clubhouse at Comrie with the Perthshire hills beyond. *Comrie Golf Club.*

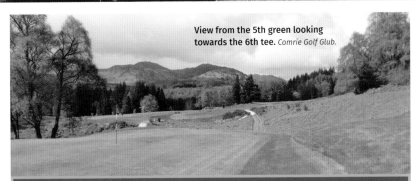

View from the 5th green looking towards the 6th tee. *Comrie Golf Glub.*

**(5) (6) SIGNATURE HOLES: PAR-3 5TH, 132–173YDS, 'HAPPY VALLEY' / PAR-5 6TH, 439YDS–493YDS, 'MONUMENT'.**

While all the holes here have their admirers, the views from the 5th and 6th will remain longest in the memory.

The par-3 5th needs plenty of club to clear a bank at the front of the green waiting to stop any ball that hits it. Wind can also be a factor here as your ball clears the treeline. Hole 6 is the only par-5. The tactic here is to keep left of the fairway with your second shot to get a clear view of the two-tier green. A 2-putt should be something to cherish at this tough hole.

front to back so any approach needs to be hitting the front. Hole 2 needs a good tee-shot over the ridge giving the right angle for an approach to a slightly raised green with bunkers at the front and trees at the back.

The first of two tough par-3s comes next. Club selection is crucial with lots of trouble in front and to the left. Missing right will still leave you chance to recover.

At the par-4 4th a good straight drive will set you up nicely for your approach shot. Aim for the left of the green to catch the bank along the side.

The final 3-hole stretch is a trio of par-4s. Hole 7 has a wide fairway but with a slope to the right can bring trouble both left and right. The 8th needs a straight drive avoiding trees either side of the fairway. Aim right with your approach to the green as it slopes to the left. The closing hole sets you up for a nerve jangling tee-shot through an avenue of trees. Use the two tall fir trees as your marker for the approach shot to the green.

**7th green at Comrie looking back towards the tee.** *Comrie Golf Club.*

# KILLIN GOLF CLUB
Killin Golf Club,
Killin,
FK21 8TX
**www.killingolfclub.co.uk**
*Phone:* +44 (0) 1567 820312
*Email:* secretary@killingolfclub.co.uk

**Essential course details –**
**Par:** 33 (White & Red tees)
**Length:** 2,296yds–2,495yds
**Longest hole:** Par-5 9th, 492yds–516yds
**Shortest hole:** Par-3 5th, 88yds–97yds
**Type:** Parkland

**Handicap Certificate:** Not required

**Green fees:**
Weekday
▼ adult 9 holes
▼ adult 18 holes
▼ junior 9 holes
▼ junior 18 holes

Weekend
▼ adult 9 holes
▼ adult 18 holes
▼ junior 9 holes
▼ junior 18 holes

▼ winter rate 9 or 18 holes (paid via honesty box)

**Caddies & equipment hire:**
£6 – clubs
£2.50 / £5 – trolley (9 holes / 18 holes)

£12 / £20 – buggy (9 holes / 18 holes)

**How do I book a round of golf?**
There are three ways to book a tee-time at Killin Golf Club:

*Online:* www.killingolfclub.co.uk (visitors booking)

*Phone:* +44 (0) 01567 820312

**Email:** clubhouse@killingolfclub.co.uk (include all relevant details – preferred dates/times, group size etc)

## HISTORY
The earliest original date golf was first played on this site is a subject that has provoked some debate. Newspaper reports suggest it may go back to June 1902, however, the R&A support a foundation date of 1911. John Duncan, a local professional, acted as adviser on a new course layout in 1913. Other than some minor alterations since, the course remains essentially the same.

## PLAYING THE COURSE
2011 saw several new tees put into operation on the course. There are now eighteen different teeing positions for men and fifteen for ladies. With different yardage, the course can have a different feel when playing twice round the 9-hole circuit.

From the par-4 1st tee keep your drive left – watch out for the burn. If you can't carry the burn aim for the middle of the fairway. For your approach shot favour the left side of the green. Hole 2 is a difficult par-3 where more club may be needed than you think. An undulating green makes for a tricky two-putt. Hole 3, another par-3, favours the right of the fairway from the tee as the contours should gather the ball to the green.

Hole 4 has blind shots off the tee and on the approach so wait for the bells to ring before making your shots over the hills.

The drive from hole 6 favours the right-side of the fairway. A bunker awaits any wayward approach shots to the right of the green. The ideal line is left of centre off the 7th tee. Bunkers guard the green both right and left but going too long could mean your ball gets wet. The par-3 8th plays longer than its yardage suggests. Avoid pitching into the ridge at the front of the green to secure a healthy score. The 9th is a long par-5 finish. Aim left of the white marker with your drive. Try and land your 2nd shot at the top of the second hill on the fairway for a clear view into the green.

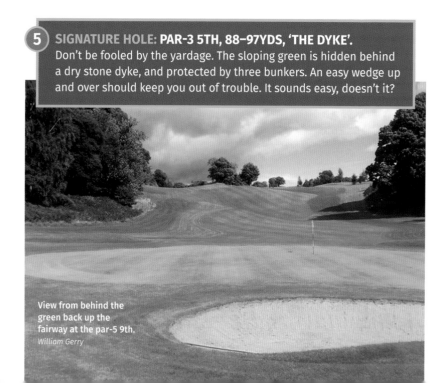

**(5) SIGNATURE HOLE: PAR-3 5TH, 88–97YDS, 'THE DYKE'.**
Don't be fooled by the yardage. The sloping green is hidden behind a dry stone dyke, and protected by three bunkers. An easy wedge up and over should keep you out of trouble. It sounds easy, doesn't it?

View from behind the green back up the fairway at the par-5 9th.
*William Gerry*

Tricky approach towards the 6th green at Killin with
Glen Lochay towering above the course. *Liz Stevens.*

# ST FILLANS GOLF CLUB

St Fillans Golf Club,
South Loch Earn Road,
St Fillans,
Perthshire
PH6 2NJ
**www.st-fillans-golf.com**
**Phone:** +44 (0) 1764 685312
**Email:** stfillansgolf@btconnect.com

---

Essential course details –
**Par:** 36* (White tees) / 37 (Red tees)
**Length:** 2,706yds–3,054yds
**Longest hole:** Par-5 2nd, 409yds–494yds
**Shortest hole:** par-3 8th, 164yds–172yds
**Type:** Inland/Parkland

---

* = Par: 34 from yellow tees (2nd hole
becomes par-4 and 6th becomes par-3)

**Handicap Certificate:** Not required

**Green fees:**
Weekday –
▼ per adult 9 holes
▼ per adult 18 holes
Juniors accompanied by paying adult
– free

Weekend –
▼ per adult 9 holes
▼ per adult 18 holes
Juniors accompanied by paying adult
– free

**Caddies & equipment hire:**
£12 – buggies (9 holes)
£18 – buggies (18 holes)
Trolleys also available upon request
Golf Clubs – free loan of half sets –
pre-book please.

**How do I book a round of golf?**
Booking is advised so as to avoid
major competition days or visiting
parties. To book a round in advance
contact the club directly (email is
preferred):

*Phone:* +44 (0) 01764 685312

*Email:* stfillansgolf@btconnect.
com (include all relevant details –
preferred dates/times, group size etc)

---

## HISTORY

St Andrews' professional and Open
Champion Willie Auchterlonie
designed St Fillans. The Countess of
Ancaster played the opening shot
on August 8 1903. Auchterlonie's
original design has been added
to over the years, increasing the
overall length to over 3,000yds from
the white tees. Sandy Lyle claims
this course to be his favourite of all
Scotland's inland courses and holds
the professional course record of 66
(18 holes).

In 2018 the club secured the

**Aerial view of the course at St Fillans on the banks of Loch Earn.** *St Fillans Golf Club.*

services of green keeper John Myles, bringing over twenty years of experience at Gleneagles to the course.

## PLAYING THE COURSE

From the white tees, with the exception of the par-5 2nd and the par-3 8th, every hole is a par-4.

Hole 1 is a slight dogleg left with a road bisecting the fairway at around 200yds. Keep your drive in the centre, avoiding the wood on the left. From here you have a clear view of the green. The 2nd is a tricky par-5. Avoid the fairway bunker with your drive and land your 2nd before a ditch in front of the green leaving a pitch up to the putting surface.

Hole 3, according to the locals, is the most 'birdie-able' hole on the course. A straight drive over heavy rough from an elevated tee followed by a wedge pitch over two bunkers protecting the front of the green and you could be in business.

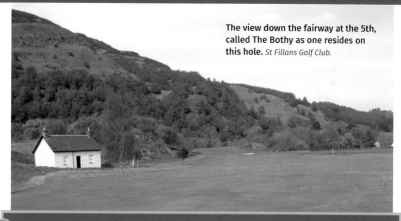

**The view down the fairway at the 5th, called The Bothy as one resides on this hole.** *St Fillans Golf Club.*

**5  SIGNATURE HOLE: PAR-4 5TH, 254–274YDS, 'THE BOTHY'.**
Strong dogleg left tempting you to take the driver out and cut off the corner. However, wind direction can play havoc with this decision. An elevated green with rough at the back means you have to be on the money with your pitch.

Hole 4 is a dogleg to the left with the line from the tee up the right side of the fairway. Be mindful of the hill on the left with your approach to the green.

Hole 6 is a straight par-4 with another clear shot for glory. The 7th is a long par-4 and regarded as the toughest hole on the course. Out of bounds on the left, trees and heavy rough to the right. If the wind blows, this hole can play very long. Hole 8 is a par-3 and quite straightforward if you avoid the bunkers either side of the green. The 9th looks like a straight drive but the best line is to the right off the tee. The approach shot needs to go over the road to a green that can be tricky to read.

At the end of your round you can enjoy the delights of the clubhouse catering, carried out by the friendliest of hosts, Julie & Jo offering their 'Nutritious and Delicious' menu for members and guests. The cake table is a sight to behold so don't be shy, tuck in!

# 9-HOLE COURSE DIRECTORY

Scotland is blessed with many other fine 9-hole courses across the country; here is a selection of those clubs that are definitely worth a look:

**Durness Golf Club**,
Durness, Sutherland
Email: lucy@durnessgolfclub.org
Website: www.durnessgolfclub.org
Phone: +44 (0) 1971 511364
**Par:** 35
**Type:** Links
**Fees:** ▼: per round

**Blair Atholl Golf Course**,
Blair Atholl, By Pitlochry
Email: info@blairathollgolf.co.uk
Website: www.blairathollgolf.co.uk
Phone: +44 (0) 1796 481552
**Par:** 35
**Type:** Parkland
**Fees:** ▼: per round

**Gairloch Golf Club**,
Gairloch
Email: via website
Website: www.gairlochgolfclub.co.uk
Phone: +44 (0) 1445 712407
**Par:** 31
**Type:** Links
**Fees:** ▼: per round / ▼: day ticket

**Tobermory Golf Club**,
Tobermory, Argyll
Email: secretary@tobermorygolfclub.com
Website: www.tobermorygolfclub.com
Phone: +44 (0) 1688 302783
**Par:** 32
**Type:** Links
**Fees:** ▼: day ticket

**Blairmore and Strone Golf Club**,
Strone, Dunoon
Email: info@blairmoregc.co.uk
Website: www.blairmoregc.co.uk
Phone: +44 (0) 1369 840676
**Par:** 31
**Type:** Parkland
**Fees:** ▼: per round

**Mearns Castle Golf Academy**,
Newton Mearns, Glasgow
Email: admin@mcgolfacademy.co.uk
Website: www.mcgolfacademy.co.uk
Phone: +44 (0) 141 644 8200
**Par:** 33
**Type:** Inland
**Fees:** ▼: per round

**Rothes Golf Club**,
Moray
Email: enquiries@rothesgolfclub.co.uk
Website: www.rothesgolfclub.co.uk
Phone: +44 (0) 1340 831443
**Par:** 35
**Type:** Inland
**Fees:** ▼: per round

**Crieff Golf Club – Dornock Course**,
Crieff
Email: bookings@crieffgolf.co.uk
Website: www.crieffgolf.co.uk
Phone: +44 (0) 1764 652397
**Par:** 32
**Type:** Inland
**Fees:** ▼: per round

**Dundas Parks Golf Club**,
Edinburgh
Email: enquiries@dundasparksgolf.co.uk
Website: www.dundasparksgolf.co.uk
Phone: +44 (0) 7787 260190
**Par:** 35
**Type:** Parkland
**Fees:** ▼: per round

**Ravelston Golf Club**,
Edinburgh
Email: via website
Website: www.ravelstongolfclub.co.uk
Phone: +44 (0) 131 315 2486
**Par:** 33
**Type:** Inland
**Fees:** ▼: per round (weekdays only)

**Kingsfield Golf Centre**,
Linlithgow
Email: info@kingsfieldgolfandleisure.co.uk
Website: www.kingsfieldgolfandleisure.co.uk
Phone: +44 (0) 1506 671607
**Par:** 34
**Type:** Inland
**Fees:** ▼: per round (weekdays & weekends)

**Paul Lawrie Golf Centre**,
Aberdeen
Email: info@paullawriegolfcentre.co.uk
Website: www.paullawriegolfcentre.co.uk
Phone: +44 (0) 1224 865750
**Par:** 27
**Type:** Inland
**Fees:** ▼: per round

**Abernathy Golf Club**,
Nethy Bridge
Email: info@abernethygolfclub.com
Website: www.abernethygolfclub.com
Phone: +44 (0) 1479 821305
**Par:** 33
**Type:** Moorland
**Fees:** ▼: per round / day ticket

**Dragon's Tooth Golf Course**,
Ballachulish
Email: info@GlencoeActivities.com
Website: www.glencoeactivities.com
Phone: +44 (0) 1855 413200
**Par:** 33 (18 separate tees for overall par of 67)
**Type:** Inland
**Fees:** ▼: day ticket

## Covesea Links,
Elgin
Email: info@covesealinks.com
Website: www.covesealinks.com
Phone: +44 (0) 1343 810012
**Par:** 31
**Type:** Links
**Fees:** ▼: day ticket

## Broadlees Golf,
Strathaven
Email: office@broadleesgolf.co.uk
Website: www.broadleesgolf.co.uk
Phone: +44 (0) 1357 300478
**Par:** 36
**Type:** Inland
**Fees:** ▼: per round (weekdays & weekends)

## Lumphanan Golf Course,
Lumphanan
Email: info@lumphanangolfclub.co.uk
Website: www.lumphanangolfclub.co.uk
Phone: +44 (0) 1339 883480
**Par:** 31
**Type:** Inland
**Fees:** ▼: per round / day ticket

## Taynuilt Golf Club,
Taynuilt
Email: via website
Website: wwwtaynuiltgolfclub.co.uk
Phone: +44 (0) 1866 822429
**Par:** 32
**Type:** Parkland
**Fees:** ▼: per round / ▼: day ticket

## Lochgilphead Golf Club,
Lochgilphead
Email: enquiries@lochgilphead-golf.com
Website: www.lochgilphead-golf.com
Phone: +44 (0) 1546 602340
**Par:** 32
**Type:** Inland
**Fees:** ▼: day ticket

## Castle Douglas Golf Club,
Castle Douglas
Email: cdgolfclub@aol.com
Website: www.cdgolfclub.co.uk
Phone: +44 (0) 1556 502801
**Par:** 34
**Type:** Parkland
**Fees:** ▼: per round